You can change your life...

"I have done a number of personal development courses, but I rate this at number 1. The reason why is because Fiona explores in depth many of the issues we struggle with, and by providing the information and practical tools on how to better manage them, gives us the opportunity to be able to live a more meaningful and purposeful life."

~ *Jenny K, Retired Nurse*

"Since doing Fi's course, I am much more in tune with my day to day and also very aware of what is in my control and what I am responsible for. I am able to look at what truly matters, not what I thought was important, work more effectively in setting up my day, align business relationships with my own values and now recognise how important it is to take the time I need for me."

~ *Lou George, Entrepreneur*

"I just completed The Steps For Change with Fiona and I have never experienced a more life changing program. The elements – like anything worthwhile – require commitment and consistency to achieve results. But Fiona's tools and delivery are so powerful that once you dive in you will be amazed by the change you see in your outlook and the shift in your mindset. This improves your life and the lives of those around you. I cannot recommend doing this program highly enough to EVERYONE."

~ *Jacquie Thomas, Flight Attendant*

"My background is in science. I am a fact-based person and I like it when things add up and make sense. Fiona is one of the people I listen to in the mindset space because she is real, honest and has specific actions that we can follow. I always feel better after talking to her and reading her content."

~ *Mel Samson, Business Owner*

"The Steps for Change Program is the best thing that I have ever done for myself and wellbeing.

I came into this group primarily for weight loss and I lost weight but what was invaluable is actually what I gained. Fiona shared her incredible knowledge and insight, giving me the tools to live my very best life. I have learnt so much about myself and others in the most incredible and supportive environment within a short amount of time. A group of people I have never met have become one of the most trusted support systems, encouraging you to be your best, keep you accountable, motivated and are there for you through your highs and lows.

Fiona has created a safe and exciting space for you to really look inside yourself, learn about how and why you do things. I feel happier, more hopeful and excited about my life and I thank God that I said yes every day! So don't hesitate to join."

~ Sarah Anderson, Marketing Manager

"I now have a deep understanding of the daily practices that keep me (and many others) in the positive and constructive mindset needed to achieve all that I want and have to. I have practical strategies that I apply both in my professional and personal life.

I have completed many leadership development programs and had Executive Coaches over my extensive Executive career and Fiona's programs and coaching stand out as some of the best, with enduring benefits and tangible outcomes."

~ Annie Volkering, Executive Director

IT IS POSSIBLE

by Fiona Redding

Letting go of who you think you are, to create the life of your dreams

IT IS
Possible

FIONA REDDING

Copyright 2023 Fiona Redding

It is Possible

Letting go of who you think you are to create the life of your dreams

thehappinesshunter.com

The information contained within this book is strictly for inspirational purposes, based on the authors observation, experience and knowledge. Should you wish to apply these practices into your life, you are taking complete and full responsibility for your actions.

No part of this book may be reproduced or utilised, in any form or by any means (electronic or mechanical), without the prior permission in writing from the publisher or author.

Disclaimer

Please note that this book is not intended to be a substitute for professional medical advice and should not be relied on as health or personal advice.

Always seek the guidance of your doctor or other qualified health professional with any questions you may have regarding your mental health or a medical condition.

Sadness passes with time. If it does not pass and is affecting the quality of your life, it could be a sign of something more, for example depression. You may want to speak with your doctor or medical practitioner before undertaking any of the recommended exercises.

Authors image: Beth Jennings

ISBN: 978-0-6452880-0-1

First Edition 2023
First published by GRABB Publishing

Dora Altintas
www.doraaltintas.com

This book is dedicated to all the masters who have gone before

THE HAPPINESS HUNTER'S INTENTION

May this be a space for connection to our heart;
for unconditional love, happiness, kindness,
acceptance, forgiveness, compassion and
peace – for ourselves, each other
and for the world.

All change begins with a decision. To say yes to you, and yes to an extraordinary life. From here, it is simply a matter of taking the next step forward, one step at a time.

Remember always, courage is not the absence of fear.

Being courageous is facing what you need to face, regardless.

And know this: as you begin to move, the Universe will rise up to meet you, every step of the way.

"As you start to walk on the way, the way appears."
~ Rumi

Content

Introduction 1

A Pivotal Moment of Awareness 5

The Big Guns 29

It is Possible 47

The Seven Elements 85

Planning for Success 111

Planting Seeds for Success 125

Mindset and Heartset 147

Celebrating your way to Success 203

The Emergency Fix 205

Tools and Resources 211

Bringing it all Together 269

A Final Word from the Author 287

Acknowledgments 289

About the Author 293

Introduction

If you told me back in 2012 that not too long into the future I would be sitting at my kitchen table looking out over the ocean, writing my second book. That I would be the creator (and co-creator) of two successful podcasts, with a company that provides training for corporations and a program that changes lives…

…*I would not have believed you.*

Because while I dearly wanted for something better in my life, my reality at the time, was that I was unemployed, overweight and incredibly unhappy. All of this, on top of a problematic drinking habit and dysfunctional relationships with people, money and myself.

I would not have believed you, because who I was then and the attitude, mindset and behaviour that kept me in that situation, to who I am, how I live and what I do now, would have seemed like an impossible dream.

Make no bones about it; there were actions that I needed to (and did) take to get me here. However, none of those steps would have mattered or yielded any results if I did not do the inner work.

I know this because before making the mindset and inner work a priority, I talked a lot about taking action - without taking action - or my action would generate a result (two steps forward), but not long after self-sabotage would set me back three steps. This pattern was true in every area of my life.

There is no doubt that the business that I love and am passionate about, which provides a monthly income more significant than my income of that year, is because I did the inner work.

The crazy thing about this, is that it was the most basic and uncomplicated practices that created this radical transformation within me, my income, health, relationships and life.

All I needed was guidance and a willingness to show up.

My purpose in writing this book is to share the tools, resources and practices that I used to make what I thought was the impossible dream a reality. And how you can too.

This guide is the book I wished I had back then.

I want you to challenge your limitations by going beyond what you think you know.

My journey from peddling in hope and wishes to life beyond my wildest dreams required me to smash down the thoughts of impossibility. It was a journey of taking the impossible to possible, and beyond.

There was a time when it seemed as though all the odds were stacked against me, despite that, I dared to dream, with the tiniest glimmer of belief. Because what I wanted at that point, seemed like an impossible dream.

It started with a "what if" and became a reality.

Making dreams come true and fulfilling wishes is a process, which is great news, because it means that anyone can achieve their dreams. It is simply a matter of following the steps and trusting the process.

"I believe it is possible, even if right now I can't see how"

I've come to learn that I get far more value from an exercise, event or meeting when I set myself an intention. What this does is set my mind, energy and focus in the right direction for the best possible outcome.

To get maximum value, have a dedicated notebook or journal to use alongside this book.

Before you read any further, take a moment to write down your biggest dreams in the areas of:

- Health and wellbeing
- Relationships - spiritual, intimate, family, friends and community
- Finances and wealth
- Business or professional development
- Adventure and play
- Education and personal development
- Charity and philanthropy

What is your impossible dream?

"A year from now you will wish you had started today".

~ Karen Lamb

A Pivotal Moment of Awareness

Life is a series of moments. Some are inconsequential and pass us by with not even a thought. And then we have those pivotal moments where there was a clearly defined before and after – where the world shifted on its axis, and things would never be the same again.

My pivotal moment came back in 2012 when on this particular day I looked around me and felt absolutely disgusted by what was before me. My moment of awareness was realising that this was a mirror of who I was at that time, representing how I was showing up. What was even more horrifying was in that moment seeing the future trajectory of my life. It was a shock to my system.

As I was walking to the kitchen, for some reason, I paused and noticed the lounge room. The paint was peeling off the scuffed walls, which had not seen a fresh coat of paint in years. The stained carpet and the shabby furniture that was clearly poorly treated. Our home environment was tense, conflicted and with a culture of blame.

When I arrived in the kitchen and seemingly noticed (for the first time) the overflowing recycling bin of empty beer and wine bottles, I realised at that moment that this was the norm of my life.

What frightened me most was the question that popped into my head– if this is where I am now, then where is my future heading?

Because if this is my now, and nothing changes, then my future is only going to get worse.

This moment of awareness was my pivotal moment: a moment of full-frontal exposure.

It is not to say this was the first moment of awareness I'd had. Let's face it, I had experienced glimpses of my reality previously and knew that this did not happen overnight. What was different this time in that moment of truth was that I fully felt and owned the situation.

The truth had hit me in the face. It was as if I could no longer look down on others and compare myself as "not so bad" to justify where I was not being, doing, living, or showing up.

We have all heard it so many times to "wake up" or "see the light"; what led me to my moment of awakening was recognising my role in the situation I found myself in.

My biggest lesson that day was finally getting this truth bomb – my external environment was a mirror of me, who I was, and how I was showing up in my life and the world. It was a challenging and profoundly confronting realisation, which brought me to my knees – emotionally, physically and spiritually.

What is Awareness?

Awareness is being fully present in the current moment, without judgement or attachment. It is seeing all that is around us – as it is.

It is devoid of resistance and is the process of observing and gathering information.

Looking back now, I recognise that for the very first time in a long time, I was present in the moment and allowed myself to experience it fully. As uncomfortable as it was, my big a-ha moment acknowledged how unhappy I was, admitting that this was not how I wanted to live.

This contrast - knowing what I did not want - allowed me to create the space to seek and explore what I did want.

While my first decision wasn't a big one, it was simply that I wanted to feel healthy and happy. It was the first of many, many decisions, and it would never have happened if I had not stopped to experience the moment, with all its discomfort.

True awareness for change is that moment that drives you to a decision to do something different.

I Am Here and Now

Being present in the moment – living in the now and with full awareness – is the most underestimated state of being regarding our personal power.

Our identity is a self-fulfilling prophecy, and studies have proven that we unconsciously create a life that reinforces our identity. The problem with this is that most of us live with our identity defined by the past.

Showing up to each day like this will only rob and deny us the opportunity to live and experience life fully.

The greatest gift of the present – devoid of attachment to the past – is the opportunity to step into the best and highest version of ourselves.

The Eagle Eye Present Moment

"Where I am now is where I am now, and where I am now is perfect."

During another dark night of the soul, I was surfing through YouTube in the early hours of the morning for content to help me find peace.

During this particular night of searching, I discovered the Eagle Eye Present Moment concept as presented by Eckhart Tolle.

I came to learn this to be the most powerful position to be present in when creating change. It has become one of the first life-changing mindset shifts I now teach my clients and students. A symbolic representation of it would be like standing in the eye of a storm – where it is calm and devoid of all the chaos and debris, and you can observe all that is.

Athletes often refer to it as being in the zone in which they operate from a higher level of awareness.

While I had heard of mindfulness and present moment awareness, I had never really grasped the concept or its impact until this particular night, when Eckhart Tolle introduced the idea of time as a horizontal and vertical axis.

He said that while we are physically here at a point in time, we are not really here because mentally and emotionally, we are either living in the past or projecting our past into our future.

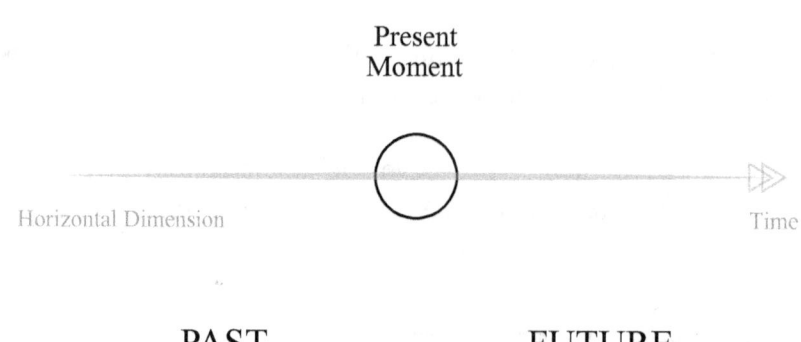

The consequences of living like this day-to-day are feelings of stagnation, being trapped, depression (stuck in the past), hopelessness, anxiety (worried about the future), anger, blame, shame, guilt etc. It is a lifecycle of being stuck in a rut or as a victim with the same patterns of drama and self-sabotage playing out repeatedly.

My lightbulb moment was recognising that I was the creator and author of what I was experiencing as a less than ideal life and circumstances, simply because I was not fully present.

This insight was incredible and exciting. Because at that moment, I understood that if what I was experiencing was a result of my creation, then I could create something different.

It was all within my power and 100% possible.

It was like someone had flicked a switch. Suddenly what was possible and what I could experience for my life took on a whole new meaning. It didn't matter what was going on at any moment in time. I always had the choice to change it.

The most incredible part about this is that it is so simple.

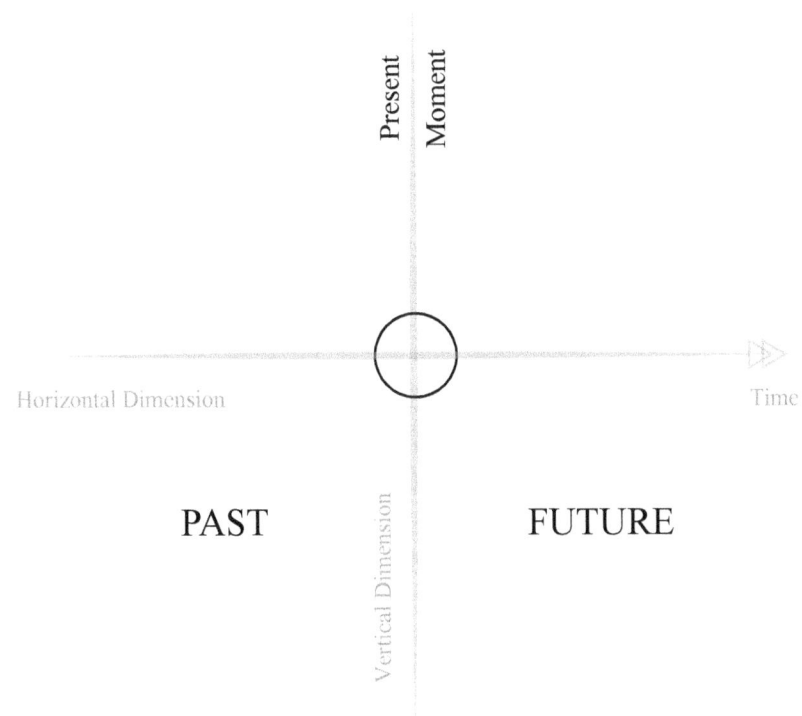

You will notice in the diagram now that vertical axis is added. Eckhart Tolle described an alternative way to think about time rather than our conditioned concept of time as linear.

He called this the vertical axis.

We are all fully engaged and immersed in this present moment on the vertical axis.

Instead of the past and future as a horizontal concept, shift your perspective to time as a vertical.

Practice this by noticing if your thoughts and emotions are in the past or future. Be aware of the narrative that is running through your mind. If you find yourself in either the past or the present, or in having an unhelpful conversation in your head, bring yourself to the present moment by focusing on your breathing and acknowledging your immediate environment.

The vertical axis is about experiencing yourself fully in the here and now and being fully present to everything within, and everyone and everything around you.

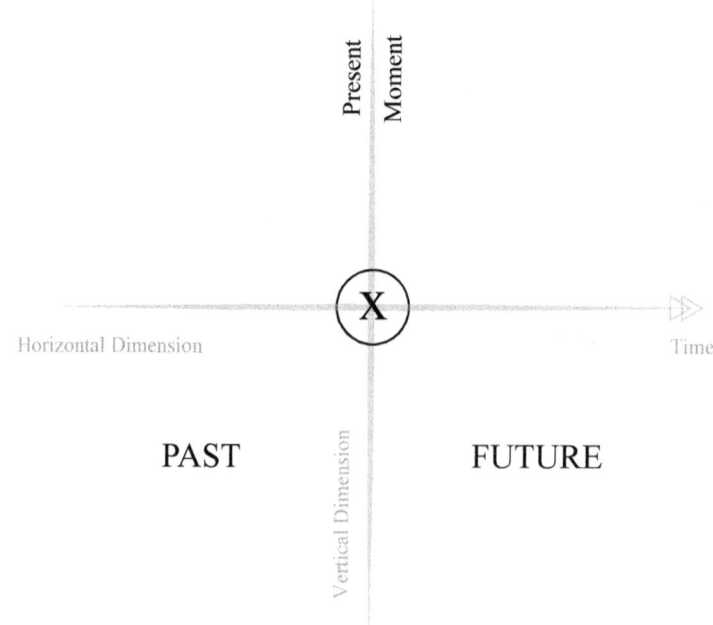

Now that you are fully present and using the diagram as your guide, move up the vertical axis to the vantage point and position of an eagle flying high above, aware and observing.

From this detached observer's perspective, you can look back over past events, decisions, and behaviour patterns to acknowledge and recognise the lessons and learnings.

When you review enough events from this position, you will start to notice patterns and common denominators.

What made this so powerful is that suddenly I had real data to work with. Quality data that would help me set up the future of my design – a future that would include all that I desired and excluding what did not serve.

In those early hours, what had started as bleakness and desolation, suddenly there was a spark of hope and a new vision of how my life could be.

I learned what was possible, that there was a pathway, and that these were the first steps.

Within 12 months, my life transformed beyond anything I could have imagined that night. And it has kept on happening.

Fiona (of back then) would be blown away if she could see the words she was writing today.

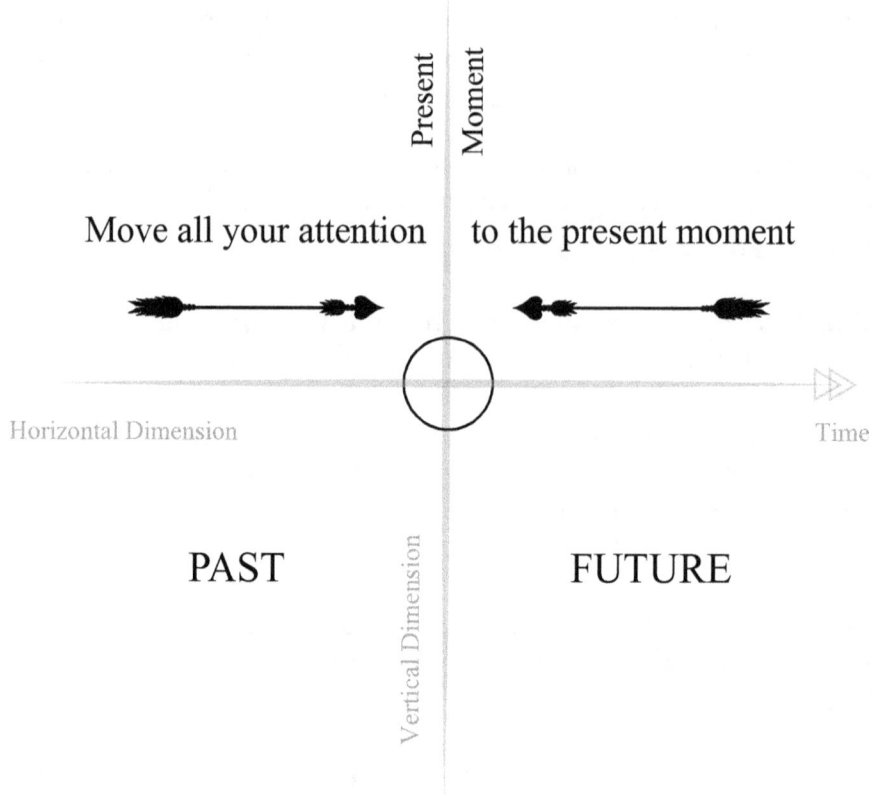

The Circle of Responsibility

"When you think everything is someone else's fault, you will suffer a lot. When you realise that everything springs only from yourself, you will learn both peace and joy."

~ The 14th Dalai Lama

The most significant difference between those who succeed in turning adversity into triumph and those who do not, is the ability to take responsibility: versus those who relinquish it onto another by pointing the finger of blame.

Here, I'm going to introduce you to the concept of radical responsibility. What I mean by this is 100% complete and absolute responsibility for your life and everything in your life and all that it entails, including seemingly innocuous events for which it doesn't even seem remotely possible for you to have any control over.

A word of warning: this can be a very confronting and challenging concept. Because taking radical responsibility will not only go against much of your existing programming, it will create physical and emotional discomfort.

It is important to remember that taking responsibility is not the same as taking the blame.

When we take 100% responsibility for our life, who we are, how we are showing up in it, what we're doing with our life – not from a place of judgement and blame, but from full and empowered responsibility – then, and only then, is where we can start to change it.

MY RESPONSIBILITY

My thoughts   My actions
My beliefs   My attitude
My emotions   My behaviour
My words   My reactions

My decisions &
their concequences

NOT MY RESPONSIBILITY

Others behaviour
Others decisions and
their consequences
Others attitude
Others thoughts
Others beliefs
Others emotions
Others words
Others actions

Taking radical responsibility starts with knowing and understanding the Circle of Responsibility and where yours starts and ends.

Imagine yourself in the centre of the circle above. The ring of the circle is the boundary of where your responsibility begins and ends.

Within this circle, the things that you have immediate control and influence over include:

- Thoughts, beliefs, attitude, effort, emotions, feelings, behaviour and actions
- The stories you tell yourself
- The decisions you make and their consequences
- The values you hold
- Your reaction and response to situations
- How you show up and what you present to the world
- How you use your time
- What you read, consume, watch, engage with and hold onto

Outside of the circle are elements that we cannot control. We cannot control what other people decide to have for dinner, what they think or how they behave.

Nobody can make us think the way we think. They cannot make us feel what we feel. How we experience life, our thoughts and feelings – these are ours to choose.

Even though it may not feel like it, we always choose how we think, feel, and respond. We always have this choice.

Knowing our Circle of Responsibility enables us to harness the power that we have within us, no longer making our experience someone else's problem.

It has been said that, if two people are in disagreement, we cannot apportion blame: like 50% responsibility here and 30% responsibility there. In communication between two people, be it conflict or a conversation, each of those is 100% involved.

The difference between the person apportioning partial responsibility and blame and someone who recognises their 100% involvement, is that they take full responsibility, while the former is in victim mode.

So this is the catch: most of us spend the majority of our time and energy outside our circle, trying to control everything else, knowing what everyone is thinking, getting upset when we don't get what we think we want, or things aren't going the way we want them to – all the while ignoring all that is within.

When we let go of the need to control our external environment and take complete and radical responsibility for our inner world, we start to see the influences and changes we desperately tried to make previously.

They seem to materialise almost as if by some miracle and feel completely effortless. This shift refers to being in the flow, in your vortex, in alignment.

I want you to know that this is a time-honoured and proven process that you can follow and achieve.

The Need to Control or be Right

When we try to control things around us, like other people or our environment, this is a safety mechanism. Our primal instinct is that when we feel under threat or feel let down, we immediately try and want to control the situation.

We do this when:

- We feel unsafe
- Fearful that things are not going our way
- The need to be right and get the last word in or prove someone wrong
- We have assumed without complete understanding or discussion

How often do you find yourself thinking any of the following thoughts?

- I know what that person is feeling
- I know why they did that
- I know what they think about me
- I know what they will say or do
- I know what they should be doing, and they are not doing it

To feel in control, often we will use these thoughts to build a case against them. Using emotions of anger, feeling let down by them or seeing them as hypocritical, lazy or judgemental.

Whereas the reality is that we have no idea what another person is thinking or why they may or may not be doing what we think they should or shouldn't be doing. We can ultimately make up something in our head that has zero truth in reality – yet holding all those around us to it as a fact.

Let's be honest. Most of the time, we don't even know in our mind what we are thinking, yet we tend to be the expert on what other people think.

We make up stories about what they think about us, we judge and criticise others, how they are living and the decisions they make, based on what we believe is the right way to be thinking or behaving.

To transform our life, we turn that lens and focus onto ourselves.

The shortfall we see in others is a mirror reflecting back to us our own.

Recognising the Need to be Right

Some examples of how our controlling behaviours present themselves:

- Helicopter parenting
- Micro-managing
- Nagging
- Being argumentative
- Lack of behavioural flexibility
- Negative overreaction to change
- Taking things personally
- Emotional manipulation
- Correcting people
- Judgement and criticism

Our most significant justification for control is that we know best, and we want the best for everyone else. The truth is that we are exerting our need to be in control or right, imposing dominance and depriving another person of their free will.

Some of these behaviours have become so automatic that you would need to stop to think about it. Digging deep into our motives to understand if this is a need to control or to be right.

Looking within and being honest about our motives is where the challenge lies. It is easy to reflect when our behaviour has a negative impact. Yet if you control other people successfully and without resistance, it is hard to see or recognise the damage to the relationship and avoid facing a weakness or problematic behaviour.

Here is the test:

- Are you able to let go of control, the need to direct and correct– without resistance or an adverse emotional reaction?
- Can you observe without uninvited input?
- Is there an internal dialogue of criticism and judgement, even though you may not be verbalising it?

If your answer was yes, maybe, or sometimes to any of these, you are playing outside your circle of responsibility.

Recognise that this is a sign of when you are at your emotional weakest and most likely to act, do or say things that could damage a relationship. Even when you have justified that the intention and act are for the greater good.

Turning the focus inwards

The solution is simple, yet in its simplicity, it is a struggle.

The action is to stop what you are doing and, in that moment, reflect on what the need to control, dominate or be right is providing you.

Notice the feelings and emotions raised when you feel that you do not control the situation versus how it feels when you feel in control.

Remember, this takes practice, and that progress outweighs perfection when it comes to getting results.

The gift is in the struggle

"Without the burden of afflictions, it is impossible to reach the height of grace. The gift of grace increases as the struggle increases."

~ St. Rose of Lima

When I look back to those moments in my life when things were not working, what stood out was how I dealt with (and avoided) life's struggles, discomfort, conflict and emotional triggers.

Back then, I viewed the struggles in my life as something that other people and circumstances created. Uncomfortable feelings were to be avoided. I felt others caused my triggers.

My method of dealing with the above was either by running away, drowning them out with destructive and distracting behaviours, or pointing the finger and blaming others.

While at the time, it gave immediate short-term relief and the avoidance of any responsibility – even though I would have point-blank denied that at the time – it didn't address the problem.

While I avoided the drama at that moment, I effectively kicked the can down the street to be stumbled across again in the near future.

Even when it had come to the point when I had decided to do something differently, I realised that I was avoiding the struggle of following through on that decision by waiting for another person to take action.

Even in this new state of wanting to do things differently, because I had avoided the struggle, the situation only got worse. For example, I was very uncomfortable talking about money, so I avoided talking about money, and my money problems worsened.

I was uncomfortable with the amount of alcohol I was drinking, so I avoided addressing the problem to justify continuing (if not to consume more). As a side note, I could fully justify my drinking because it was the only way I felt like I could cope with what I thought my life had become.

In other words, I avoided dealing with the discomfort. I had become very good at avoiding things.

Here is what happens when you make a daily living out of avoiding things. At some point, things will hit the fan, and it feels as if life is slapping you around the head so hard that you no longer have the false luxury of being able to avoid it.

And this moment came for me when every area of my life seemed to implode in a very short space of time. While it felt like it happened overnight, I now know that this was in the making for years as I had consistently avoided dealing with anything that made me feel uncomfortable.

Forced to face the situation head on and take action (despite the fear and discomfort), it flicked a switch in me – *it changed my life*. For the first time, I felt the strength and gift of embracing the struggle.

What I learned back then, and have continued to learn and confirm (including up until today!) is that there are two significant gifts of embracing struggles, emotional discomfort and triggers.

As strange as it may seem, the first gift is the gift of having your weaknesses exposed. Because, like the eagle eye position, you now have quality data to work with towards a solution.

Taking the time and making an effort to look at the thoughts, emotional reactions and behaviours which keep you stuck, are how you turn adversity and weaknesses into your greatest strengths.

Time and time again, we see countless examples of adversity being turned into strength throughout history, in the Bible and other spiritual texts, through fables, sport, business and entertainment. For this to have happened, the weakness needed to be exposed and overcome.

The second gift is discovering the previously unknown strength and power within. It is only in moments of adversity and testing that people realise their untapped strength.

Diamonds form under pressure. Once uncovered, they are cut and polished to their brilliance. Gold takes its shape under unimaginable heat.

Be it a weakness or strength exposed or illuminated, think of it as a diamond in the rough that now needs polishing and effort to shine to its full brilliance.

Fast forward to today, I still face discomfort, struggles and triggers. The difference is that I have come to learn to celebrate and embrace those times for what they are – opportunities and signs of growth.

We have all heard of growing pains. Whether it be business, health, relationships or finances, recognise that you will continue to face challenges that will either stop your progress or launch you into the next phase of growth.

Life is a series of obstacles and challenges. Overcoming them is a part of the great adventure; this is what life is and what living is all about. It is here that we find true happiness and meaning. I have come to embrace that these challenges are a sign and an early indicator of success. This insight is why I now see challenges as opportunities.

A word of warning about our struggles and challenges – they are sneaky!

We need to be vigilant in remembering that what we are struggling with belongs to us and ultimately nothing to do with anyone else. Any challenge we have with anything or anyone external to us is simply a mirror reflecting what lies within, even though we might not want to admit it.

It takes courage to own our stuff.

The Teflon Strategy

This amazing little strategy I implemented during a particularly challenging time in my life. I wanted to create a different relationship between myself and all those around me.

If I wanted a different outcome, I had a better chance of achieving it if I took responsibility for how I showed up.

I wanted to be empowered and eliminate negative emotional reactions.

I was sick of feeling like a victim and wanted to be back in the driver's seat of my life. I knew that I wanted to learn to manage myself and my emotions better.

I wanted to be a RESPONDER, not a REACTOR.

So, I started visualising myself as Teflon, and I started affirming - "I am Teflon".

And whenever I felt like I was being attacked or judged or any other negative thing, I accepted this feeling was my stuff and nothing to do with another.

When we are highly emotional in situations, we cannot understand or empathise with another person's viewpoint, as all of our energy focuses on dealing with what is happening within.

None of us can ever honestly know another person's emotional state or thought process. This is especially true when we are unable to step into their shoes without adding our story to the situation, or seeing it through our lens and filter.

Truthfully, most of the time, we don't even know where we are ourselves in our minds, but we are always the expert on another person, what they are thinking and why (right?).

To move through this, I practised seeing myself as Teflon: just letting whatever I perceived as being thrown at me to simply slide off.

It would not stick.

It allowed me to move into a place where I could choose how to respond rather than react.

It allowed me to choose how to respond in one of four ways:

> 1. To let it go completely – to let it go through to the keeper. It was not mine, and I did not want it.
>
> 2. To consider the spoken words. To reflect on the information presented. Was there truth or merit to it, and if so, what was I going to do with that? What different choices or actions could I be taking?
>
> Here was my clue, if what was said triggered an emotional reaction within me, I knew that it was something that needed my attention.
>
> 3. To communicate from a calm and clear space with an objective and goal to resolve the issue. Recognising that when we act from a highly emotional state, we ALL behave in ways that are not always reasonable.
>
> 4. To practice cutting the other person some slack.

By taking responsibility for how I showed up, instead of focusing on what the other person was or was not doing suddenly created the space to communicate differently.

This strategy is excellent to use in any area of your life in which you feel attacked. Whereas developing the skill set of setting boundaries will diminish or avoid these perceived attacks in the first place.

Boundaries

Boundaries are the emotional limits set, which are activated when breached. A breach is usually a behaviour or a comment which violates a personal value.

The breaches could be concerning requests for your time and how another treats and speaks to you or invades your personal space.

Even though you may not know what a boundary is, you know it has been crossed when you have an instant and uncomfortable emotional reaction.

Most people have set their boundaries unconsciously, and in a world of healthy relationships, these are generally sufficient. However, when it comes to unhealthy environments, relationships or poor communication, the lack of awareness and strength of the boundaries is where the challenges arise.

Why do we need them?

A person with weak or non-existent boundaries is frequently surrounded by drama, whether it is their own or not. They feel unappreciated and used.

Without boundaries, people are inefficient with their time; often describing themselves as time-poor.

They are scattered with their thoughts and actions, with action initiated by looming deadlines rather than proactive effort.

On the extreme end of weak or lack of boundaries, stress is a close and frequent companion.

The person with solid boundaries is confident about who they are and how they show up. They are less likely to experience energy depletion or drain.

The Myths and Truths of Boundaries

Myth – Energy vampires

In the book by J.K Rowling, Harry Potter and the Prisoner of Azkaban, we were introduced to soulless creatures known as the dementors. These are a phantom species who deprive human minds of happiness and intelligence.

While it is rare that we will ever come across a person that could completely drain us of life and happiness in a moment, we can meet people who leave us feeling less energised after an interaction.

Empaths are people who are more tuned in to the energy of their surroundings and people. It is considered an intuitive trait.

The myth of being an empath is that one is highly susceptible to negative energy and can't control it, except to remove themselves from the environment.

FACT: Optimal energetic flow within will deflect the negative energy of another

The strength and health of your energy flow is your boundary in these situations. Think of it in the same way as you would think about your body's immune system.

A healthy immune system deflects and deals with viruses without you even knowing about it. A depleted immune system is susceptible to the weakest of viruses.

Just like we make sure that we support our immune system with healthy activities such as plenty of sleep, good nutrition and mindfulness, the same tools apply to our energetic health.

Myth – Boundaries are selfish

Once you put boundaries in place, it is common to find yourself feeling selfish or accused of being selfish.

Being called selfish will often sting a person who is new to setting boundaries. This discomfort happens because they feel they are letting people down.

Saying no does not mean that you do not care about others. It can mean that you are saying no because you do care.

You serve yourself and another by holding you both to a higher standard of interaction. In these situations, remind yourself of the bigger picture for yourself and all included.

Myth – Boundaries are permanent

A trap that most fall into when setting boundaries for the first time is to believe that they are fixed and permanent. It is not the case.

A boundary follows the same philosophy of behavioural flexibility: having the emotional intelligence to know when to hold, flex, or adjust according to your circumstances.

It may take a little practice to learn, and you may not always get it right, particularly in the early days. However, keep the faith because I promise you that you will get there - and it will be worth it.

How to Set and Use Boundaries

Boundaries are a sign of self-respect, so love yourself enough to set and honour them. They come in many forms, and most conversations refer to emotional boundaries of how we allow others to treat or speak to us. Yet, we tend to overlook the boundaries we set, or do not set, for ourselves.

Setting a wake-up and bed-time is a boundary that we set for ourselves. Creating a meal plan that we adhere to, or committing, following through and completing a task are other boundaries.

Boundaries are more than about how others treat you; it is about how you treat you.

Know your limits

You cannot set a boundary if you don't know where you stand.

Listen to your gut

Practice self-awareness, as your emotions and feelings will let you know when a boundary has been crossed.

Do it with grace

Your boundaries are your boundaries. Don't make it someone else's problem or someone else's job to manage, and avoid blaming others for the need to set them. This decision is your choice. Own it.

Set them with grace and quietly (e.g. you can avoid unsolicited preaching of your new boundaries).

Expect that if you set a significant boundary where there has not previously been one, you may get a reaction from others. Be kind, practice empathy and understand that they are also going through a learning curve of adjustment.

Review them regularly

As we evolve, so do our needs. Make a note to check-in if your current boundaries are meeting your needs, and adjust accordingly.

The Big Guns

I realised that my life was not what I wanted, and at the same time, I understood that I had created my current situation. I knew I had the power to create the life I wanted.

Up until this point, I had learned how I was contributing to this situation and had gained an awareness of the behaviour I needed to stop fuelling the issues in my life.

The question now was: *"What did I have to start doing instead?"*

It really came down to three key actions, which I now refer to as The Big Guns.

And they are called The Big Guns, because it is here where the power lies. With The Big Guns in your arsenal, you can overcome anything.

Following awareness with these three steps, creates the space for the ultimate transformation.

Essentially, this is how The Big Guns work. We gain awareness. We accept where we are. We forgive ourselves and everyone else for being here, and we find something to appreciate within the awareness. Praise and thanksgiving by its very nature energises us. From this more enlightened perspective, we can begin to create change.

The Big Guns allow us to come to peace with who we are and where we are, in the present moment.

Acceptance

I first discovered this idea of acceptance as a practice when I came across Louise Hay's work and her affirmation: "I love and accept myself unconditionally."

Louise's process was to write these words on a post-it note and put it on a mirror. For 30 days you speak them out loud, twice a day as you look into your eyes in the mirror. This is called "mirror work".

I felt empowered because I had taken some big and scary first steps, which had pushed through the fear barrier that had up until that point stopped me from taking any action. It was almost like breaching an invisible wall that I did not ever think I would be able to cross.

In the absence of blaming others, the decision was made to take responsibility for my life. I was suddenly faced with who I was, and what I thought and felt about myself. It was not pretty.

The self-talk was confronting. I would never speak to my worst enemy in the way I was speaking to myself. This harmful and nasty chatter was the constant dialogue in my head. Not only was it creating self-doubt about the future, but it was also dragging me back into the past with anger and blame towards others, and thoughts of guilt and shame about all the things I had done wrong and all the time I had wasted.

In a nutshell, even though I had an awareness of my current situation, the reality was that I was not fully accepting the situation for what it was. I was not accepting where I was. I was not accepting myself.

Listening to Louise in the early hours of the morning, I heard a calm, gentle, motherly voice tell me that there was nothing wrong with me. It was spoken with such love, reminding me that I was perfect just the way I was.

When it came to my self-talk or the talk from others that I acknowledged about me, I realised that I had never heard this level of love or respect. I say "acknowledged" because while there were loving and supporting friends and family in my life, I realised that I was only hearing those who were matching or confirming my self-talk. I rejected love.

In that moment of seeking a better way to do things, I realised that my current self-talk would keep me stuck, and I needed to change the tune.

It was evident that this acceptance and affirmation practice was my next big step.

The following morning, I wrote the affirmation: "I love and accept myself unconditionally", and placed the post-it note on my bathroom mirror.

Then I stood there, staring at myself in the mirror, feeling very self-conscious. I spoke the words for the first time. I felt awkward and uncomfortable. Despite this, I repeated the process later that day and continued twice daily.

I decided this was my anchor. If my thoughts veered off course or back into the past, or if I was giving myself or others a tough time, this was my go-to response. I discovered that the Fiona who spoke those words was loving, caring, understanding and gentle.

And this brings me to the crucial elements of why this practice is so powerful.

First, it is removing the need to label a situation as wrong or right – it simply is what it is, hence our Happiness Hunter affirmation of:

"Where I am now is where I am now. And where I am now is perfect."

We do this because it eliminates resistance; there is no trying to wish that something was different or it wasn't as it was.

It is literally just saying, here I am, I am here, and I accept it.

> I am not going to try to defend my position here.
>
> I am not going to try to justify it.
>
> I am not going to wish that something was different.
>
> I am not going to complain about it.
>
> I am not going to blame anybody for it.
>
> I am just going to accept my thoughts and the way I feel.

To let go of everything else around me, that I am here, and this is where I am.

In doing this, we position ourselves in a better place to think and feel differently about where we are.

We can look forward and be open to the next step from a completely new and empowered perspective.

Remember, before you speak the words "I love and accept myself unconditionally", step into the role of a loving parent or your most caring self.

I cannot stress enough how important it is to feel the love and support behind these words, especially when coming from you and from within.

Last but not least, and this is what I really believe was the core foundation of my success – I was doing this with absolute sincerity. I was showing up 100% for me.

Emotionally, financially and physically, I had my back against the wall; this wasn't just my life on the line. It was the lives of my children. And while I wasn't aware of it at the time, looking back now, I can see that this wasn't just a checklist I was working through.

It was a non-negotiable fight for a new life.

This attitude of taking no prisoners, of showing up to do the work fully present, emotionally and mentally, is the secret ingredient to seeing results.

Forgiveness

So there I was, several weeks into this new daily practice. Diligently practising the mirror work of loving and accepting myself unconditionally and starting to see and experience some significant shifts within me and in my relationships.

Relationships that were once filled with conflict, blame and dysfunction, were calmer, more respectful and heading in the direction of working together towards common goals.

While it seemed these shifts were magical, I also recognised them because my affirmations shifted my internal dialogue, which influenced the way I felt, which then impacted the way I showed up in my relationships.

I was now starting to get a real taste of what I had been yearning for. While the shifts were a massive improvement on where I was before, I also knew that I was only just getting a taste of what was possible. I wanted more.

I became a believer and further committed to this process.

By removing the layers of a poor attitude towards my life, I had uncovered underlying feelings of intense anger and blame towards others, coupled with feelings of guilt and shame towards myself, with a good dash of bitterness thrown in.

I was ready for the next step. This is where forgiveness came into play.

> *"To forgive is to set a prisoner free and discover that prisoner was you."*
>
> *~ Louis B Smedes*

Like many of my students and clients, my initial reaction to the practice of forgiveness was a sense of massive resistance: that I just could not do it.

When I first introduce the practice of forgiveness, a typical response is a strong reluctance to let go of the anger. Especially when the anger and bitterness have been a driving force in moving forward. A misplaced emotion.

When we take on the role of judge, jury and prosecutor, it is easy for us to decide that a wrong has been committed. This is also part of the need to be right and to control behaviour.

This is a hard one to shift and where the agreement of being a Happiness Hunter comes into play. Even if it makes no sense and you feel resistance and you don't want to do it, you just do it by taking action in faith, holding the vision and trusting the process.

What is forgiveness?

In its simplest form, forgiveness is about releasing past hurts and anger. We do it by letting go of our need to hold someone to judgement (making ourselves, another or the event right or wrong).

How to Forgive

Forgiveness starts with a decision.

What I have found to be the most successful method, and what we use in The Happiness Hunter, is the Ho'oponopono forgiveness technique.

> Ho'oponopono is a Hawaiian practice of reconciliation and forgiveness. The Hawaiian word translates into English simply as a correction.
>
> It is about putting rights, amending and tidying up. It is also considered a mental cleansing. In Hawaiian culture, it involves family conferences where relationships are set right through prayer, discussion, confession, repentance, mutual restitution, and forgiveness.

Journal Exercise

1. Give yourself time and space.

2. On a blank piece of paper, make a list of events, memories and people who you feel wronged by and those you've wronged.

3. Go to the mirror, look yourself in the eye. For each memory, look directly into your eyes and repeat the phrase until you can no longer feel the emotional charge to the memory.

4. "I'm sorry. Please forgive me. I love you. I thank you."

5. Repeat for a minimum of three times for each memory, and then draw a line through the memory to cross it out.

6. Burn the paper outside, in the sink or saucepan (careful not to burn down the house!).

Note: Burning is optional, and in reality, has no impact on the efficacy of the exercise. The true power of forgiveness comes through the feeling within yourself as you allow yourself to let go.

As the paper burns, repeat the forgiveness mantra - "I'm sorry. Please forgive me. I love you. I thank you."

Note: Some students like to bury the ashes as part of their closure process.

7. Journal (write) your feelings.

In the Tools and Resources chapter, we cover the powerful practice of decluttering your physical environment. What is to be noted here is that forgiveness is the ultimate in mental and emotional decluttering.

> "Holding onto anger is like drinking poison and expecting the other person to die."
>
> ~ *Buddha*

Gratitude

Before I practised acceptance, forgiveness and gratitude, my view of the world was always from the perspective and mentality of the victim.

Acceptance helped me be okay with what is, and forgiveness released me from the emotional shackles of the past.

What remained was to shift my scarcity and lack of mindset to recognising the opportunity, wealth and goodness that was already present in my life.

Gratitude was the solution.

My gratitude practice started off very basic and simple, and that was to be happy and grateful for my life.

Being grateful that I had a house to live in (that I could clean).

Being grateful that I lived in a country with access to clean water and health care.

Being grateful for my family.

Being grateful for a full tank of petrol, which is still one of my ultimate anchors of abundance.

Being grateful that I now understood how important being grateful was.

Like most coming into this practice, I realised that gratitude is the celebration of all that I am and all that I have. However, things really took off on a whole new level when I came to understand that gratitude, when done right, becomes the practice to summon forth and claim future goals and desires as a done deal.

The Happiness Hunter, the podcast, books and programs; I was celebrating this business, what it allowed me to do, the clients and the income that gave me financial freedom all the way back in 2013 (at a time when I was homeless and financially struggling).

Let's face it, we don't say thank you for things we will receive. We say thank you for what we have already received.

Showing gratitude for The Happiness Hunter and all that it encompassed created a shift in my identity. I became the person who leads and runs a very successful, purposeful, fulfilling and highly profitable business.

A business with global impact. Instead of a person with no capital trying to start a business without any real idea of what she is doing.

There is a big difference in how we show up energetically when the result is a given instead of a maybe. There is a big difference in the energy and presence of a person **trying** to do something compared to a person who has already done it.

What is Gratitude?

> *"A grateful heart is a magnet for miracles."*
>
> ~ unknown

Gratitude is the act of appreciation and celebration of an event, person or thing.

It is important to note that the most significant benefit comes from the process of being grateful rather than the object of our appreciation. Gratitude retrains our minds to focus and look for all that is good by default.

When we think better thoughts, we feel better. When we feel better, we think better thoughts. A lack and scarcity-focused mindset tends to only see lack and scarcity; making us feel bad. And on it goes.

We always have an abundance of gifts and blessings to appreciate, no matter what the situation.

Being grateful has the power to:

- Change the way you see and experience situations, people and events
- Build resilience
- Rewire the brain's neural pathways

- Eliminate stress
- Improve relationships
- Boost self-esteem
- Enhance emotional states
- Improve financial circumstances

My belief is that there are two focuses for gratitude.

The first is to shift your perspective in the present moment to what is already there instead of what is missing. To focus on the cup half full.

The second is where it really comes into its full power and creation. This is where we own and claim our desired outcomes as a done deal.

How to Practice Gratitude

Daily gratitude practice for an attitude readjustment

I recommend doing your gratitude practice first thing in the morning (after your meditation), as it is a great way to set your energy and focus on all the good and great things in your life.

Task: In your gratitude journal, write out at least 10 things for which you are grateful.

Remember to include the emotion or the feeling as to why you are grateful. Be sincere in your gratitude practice, fully present and playing all out. This will make a big difference as to how fast you experience the results (the effects of which can be immediate and permanent).

For those who have experienced long-term pain and/or operated from a negative perspective, it can be pretty challenging to find the simplest of things to be grateful for. I recall how hard it was to see the good in anything when my attitude was that of a victim. I started with something small.

My practice started with acknowledging and appreciating the simplest of things. Things like the chair I was sitting on. The air I was breathing. Hugs with my children. Waking up to another day. And having another moment to reset or do things differently.

No matter how bleak things feel, this process is so important. Allow yourself the time to find something to appreciate.

Gratitude practice for claiming your goals and desires

Remember, we don't say thank you for things we are about to receive. We say thank you for what we have already received. So when practicing gratitude, speak and feel as though you have received and are celebrating at that moment.

The power is in the feeling you evoke during the practice. The power is not in words you don't believe.

To cement and declare your intention for the day, speak out loud the following:

Today is a great day

I am calm

I am open to abundance in all of its forms

Thank you for this amazing day

Thank you for my incredible life

Thank you for the all of the people in my life to love and care for

Thank you for my clear and focused mind

Thank you for my open and grateful heart

Thank you for my strong and healthy body

Thank you for my loving and willing service

Thank you for all of the wonderful opportunities coming my way today

Thank you for today

Like guided meditations, affirmations and mantras are a perfect guide for the beginner. With practice and through consistency, you will find your own voice.

Whether you use a quote or your own words, the key here is to speak with feeling and absolute belief.

> "The more thankful I became, the more my bounty increased.
> That's because for sure – what you focus on expands.
> When you focus on the goodness in life,
> you create more of it."
>
> ~ Oprah Winfrey

It is Possible

At the end of 2020, my friend Kirst sent me a photo taken almost nine years prior. My focus over the last few years has been to move and face forward. I rarely look back.

Yet when I looked at that photo, what I saw and was reminded of, was the immense level of pain and hopelessness that I lived with. I felt a deep sense of sadness for the woman that was me in the photo. I just wanted to reach back and let Fiona in the photo know how much I love her and how loved she really was.

I wanted to tell her that everything was going to be alright; in fact, better than alright. To let her know that in just over 12 months from that moment, she would make the decision that would forever change the course of her life.

That she would decide what she was currently accepting as to how she lived would no longer be acceptable, and that she would be prepared to do whatever it took to change.

That she would choose happiness for her life.

I wanted her to know that she would become the person who dared to say yes to herself, that was courageous enough to trust that it was safe to take a step into the unknown. And to keep taking those steps into the unknown, moving forward, often terrified, knowing deep within that this was the way.

That she would connect to and embrace the power within to bring forth and manifest all her desires.

I remember the exact moment when the photograph was taken. I remember thinking that this was the best position in life that I could have, and I honestly thought that this was it. This was my life, and I just needed to suck it up and get on with it.

At the time the photograph was taken, I was:

- A mum of two toddlers (not quite one and three years of age)
- Unemployed and financially stressed
- Drinking and smoking was a big part of my day (the picture was of me with a beer in my hand)
- Depressed and anxious
- Struggling with all of my relationships
- Unbelievably unhappy
- Lacking any level of confidence or belief in myself
- Operating with an underlying feeling of anger
- Feeling trapped and staring down the barrel of my future life
- Unfit, overweight (over 90 kgs) and unhealthy, with early indicators of health issues. I felt horrible and uncomfortable in my body, yet at the same time, I was in absolute denial

As I was to come to understand, I had created this, which meant that I could do something about it. And this was powerful knowledge for me. If I had created this for my life, then I could create anything.

Since the image was taken in 2011, in every way, my life has completely transformed.

Today:

- I do not drink alcohol and have not had a drink since January 2013
- I have loving, thriving and positive relationships
- I am the fittest, healthiest and happiest I have ever been (lost 30kgs and kept it off)
- I operate and show up from a position of empowered living and have people, tools and practices to support me
- I built a business from the ground up, helping other people change their lives, teaching all which I have learned and implemented in my own life
- I have written and published two books
- I am the host of two podcasts
- I live debt-free
- I have reconnected with my faith, which brings me untold peace and joy

I took a stand for me.

This is the promise I made to myself.

Dear Fiona,

I love you and my greatest wish for you is to be happy and healthy and to have the most amazing and magnificent life that you possibly can.

Because I love you and want only the best for you, from this date forward I am choosing to:

Draw a circle around myself and take complete responsibility for everything within that circle. My internal dialogue and judgements. How I speak to others, the quality of my thoughts, integrity of my actions and questioning of my beliefs.

Of being selective about who is within and outside the circle. I am mindful of how I spend my time. Of what I say yes or no to, and of being aware of what is going on for me in this present moment.

I accept 100% responsibility for what is in my life and what is not in – I no longer blame others or adopt a victim mentality. I choose to be empowered in all ways.

I am crystal clear on what I want for my life, where I am heading and how I want to be living and I give myself permission to be that person and live that life every single day.

I do the work required every day to manifest my beautiful life.

I live in the present moment.

I remind myself every day that happiness is my right.

I choose happiness in every moment, because this is the greatest gift I can give myself, my loved ones, and the world.

Love Fiona

Seeing the Illusion

In the book: "The Republic, Plato's 'Allegory of the Cave'" the nature of belief versus knowledge is discussed.

In the allegory, there are prisoners chained together in a cave since childhood, unable to move their heads except to face forward. Behind the prisoners is a fire, and between the fire and the prisoners are people carrying puppets or other objects.

This casts a shadow on the other side of the wall. The prisoners watch these shadows, believing them to be the true reality – not realising they are simply seeing the reflection of what is behind them.

Plato imagines that one prisoner frees himself, finally seeing the illusion and reality of the creation of the shadows on the wall.

Once free, the prisoner looked around and saw that the fire cast the distorted shadows of the caravan of people walking along a roadway. Some carrying objects, some talking; the flame distorted the shadows cast which did not even look like the real people.

The prisoner follows the pathway and steps into the light of the world outside the cave.

He returns to tell his fellow prisoners about the world beyond the shadows, to free them from the illusion. They fought back in defence of what they believed to be the truth, based entirely on what they could see.

The allegory demonstrates and speaks to the vast realm of knowledge and reality beyond our own self-created caves. Watching the shadows on the wall, believing them to be the truth and willing to defend them no matter what.

What we see presented before us is not always what is. Yet, not everybody is ready or willing to look beyond this.

The Allegory of Fiona's Cave

Earlier, I shared how I wanted to reach back to Fiona of 2011 and tell her of all the fantastic things she would achieve, including beyond what she could even comprehend then.

I wanted to tell Fiona, who at the time felt disgusted with her physical body and struggled to keep any kind of effort towards health and nutrition, that she would not only be at her ideal body weight, but would be active, healthy, and so in love with life and herself.

I wanted to tell the woman holding all around her as emotional hostages (by blaming them for her behaviour and anger) that she would receive regular messages from clients full of gratitude for her teachings; telling her of the massive changes they were creating in their lives, families, finances and businesses.

I wanted her to know that it would be her journey to overcome the now, that would inspire, provide hope for, and give courage to others to do the same.

I wanted to tell her that she would earn more in a single month consistently than she had in all of that year.

But, here's the thing. When I positioned myself to have this conversation, to tell Fiona of the wonderful things in store for her – instead of hope or joy or excitement, I was surprised to be met with a blank wall of nothing.

I could not connect with her; and the more I tried, the bigger the resistance. It wasn't long after this that I felt a wave of rising anger, and at that moment, I realised that it wouldn't have mattered what I tried to tell Fiona in 2011 – she was too angry to listen.

There was a big disconnect to the possibility of anything outside of the deep hole she believed was absolutely true. There was no rational thinking, let alone hearing anything outside of her own looping story.

Anything I would have said to her about the here and now would have been impossible. And if in actual fact, I had a time machine to go back in time and tell her this, she would have taken the opposite action, just to prove the impossibility of it all.

That Fiona was a willing prisoner of a cave and reality of her own making, and at that time, she would have defended it at all costs.

I can give you all the tools, the step-by-step action plans, the meditation guides and resources. I can champion and support you, encouraging you to aim higher and dream bigger. However, you must be willing to have faith and consider a reality beyond what you currently know for any of that to happen by:

- Putting aside all that you believe to be true, for what is
- Not knowing what comes after a decision, but making it anyway

This first step is a decision that only you alone can make.

I will ask you to do things that may not make sense, and while there may be an explanation as to why we are doing something or the benefits, there will come a time when you may question or doubt the purpose.

Know that this is a test of your faith and commitment to wanting something better for yourself. Hold the vision, trust the process and keep going.

Faith believes that you are worth it, even when you don't.

Faith is about following through and taking action, even when it makes no sense.

Faith is holding the vision and trusting the process, when all appears to be in disarray.

What does it mean to live a life of possibility?

To understand what living a life of possibility means, we need to understand the concept of possibility. And to do that, let's first start with an impossible mindset.

A fixed, deflective position leaves very little room or receptiveness for growth. It's a "that will never happen", "tell them they're dreaming" attitude.

Showing up each day with a mindset and attitude of possibility is simply embracing that it may happen. That no matter how big or ridiculous the vision or goal may seem, all you need to do is accept that it is possible.

*"To one who has faith, no explanation is necessary.
To one without faith, no explanation is possible."*

~ Thomas Aquinas

Success

"If you want a thing bad enough to go out and fight for it, to work day and night for it, to give up your time, your peace and sleep for it.

If all that you dream and scheme is about it, and life seems useless and worthless without it.

If you gladly sweat for it and fret for it and plan for it and lose all your terror of the opposition for it.

If you simply go after that thing that you want with all your capacity, strength and sagacity, faith, hope and confidence and stern pertinacity.

If neither cold, poverty, famine, nor gout, sickness nor pain, of body and brain, can keep you away from the thing that you want.

If dogged and grim you besiege and beset it, with the help of God, You will get it!"

~ Berton Braley

Living with a Major Definite Purpose

"He who has a why to live can bear almost any how."

~ Friedrich Nietzsche

Author Napoleon Hill (Think and Grow Rich) believes that we need a Major Definite Purpose because it helps us develop self-reliance, personal initiative, imagination, enthusiasm and self-discipline.

It represents a burning desire within us, yearning to be realised and materialised. A desire so strong that we can literally move mountains because of the strength and clarity of vision we hold within.

When we consistently affirm our Major Definite Purpose, we program our subconscious mind to see and create opportunities.

Our Major Definite Purpose becomes a significant part of our identity.

The framework for developing and realising your Major Definite Purpose is quite simple.

You need to decide what you want, getting really clear about what you are asking for. Then you set a date by which it will be achieved. You need to determine what you are willing to do in exchange for what you want, what you are willing to sacrifice (nothing comes from nothing). Then make an imperfect overarching plan of how you will do it.

Your Major Definite Purpose is a concise written statement which includes these details. Then you read it out loud daily until you are taking the right action and achieving the results – fully stepping into this new identity.

7th January 2019

"I, Fiona Rachel Redding, have realised my fullest potential.

I am Australia's most successful female entrepreneur.

In return, I have built, inspired, led and nurtured a global community. I have created innovative, ground-breaking, practical and useful strategies, programs and services. Giving the best of my knowledge and experience to individuals and organisations seeking a happier, more balanced, connected and meaningful life.

Starting in 2019 and building on the previous work I have done and relationships I have developed, I have achieved international awareness and recognition. From then onwards until the end of 2029, I have in my possession over 200 million dollars.

I live my life in the way I please, in accordance with God's will for my life, and I have achieved inner peace and harmony."

Fiona ♡

A little note about "being realistic".

Reality and being realistic is what you decide it is. As tempting as it is to down play your version of reality based on another person's version or judgement, I am here to remind you that the only truth that matters is the one you believe is possible for you.

Having 200 million dollars in my bank account is an absolute reality and fact as far as I am concerned. Money is simply the physical representation that I have expanded to attract, receive and sustain that level of energy. It opens up my thinking and it charges up my actions. It feels limitless and expansive.

> *"Until one is committed, there is hesitancy, the chance to draw back, always ineffectiveness.*
>
> *Concerning all acts of initiative and creation, there is one elementary truth, the ignorance of which kills countless ideas and splendid plans: that the moment one definitely commits oneself, then providence moves too.*
>
> *All sorts of things occur to help one that would never otherwise have occurred. A whole stream of events issues from the decision, raising in one's favour all manner of unforeseen incidents, meetings, and material assistance which no man could have dreamed would have come his way."*
>
> *~ William Hutchison Murray*

Ikigai

Another way of thinking about purpose is to explore the Japanese concept of Ikigai. It is powered by a deeper, more expansive interpretation of happiness than the "follow your passion" ethos that we more commonly subscribe to in the west. Finding your Ikigai necessitates a deep and often lengthy search of self.

Think of your Ikigai as the space where what you love, what you care about, what the world needs and what you can get paid for, meet.

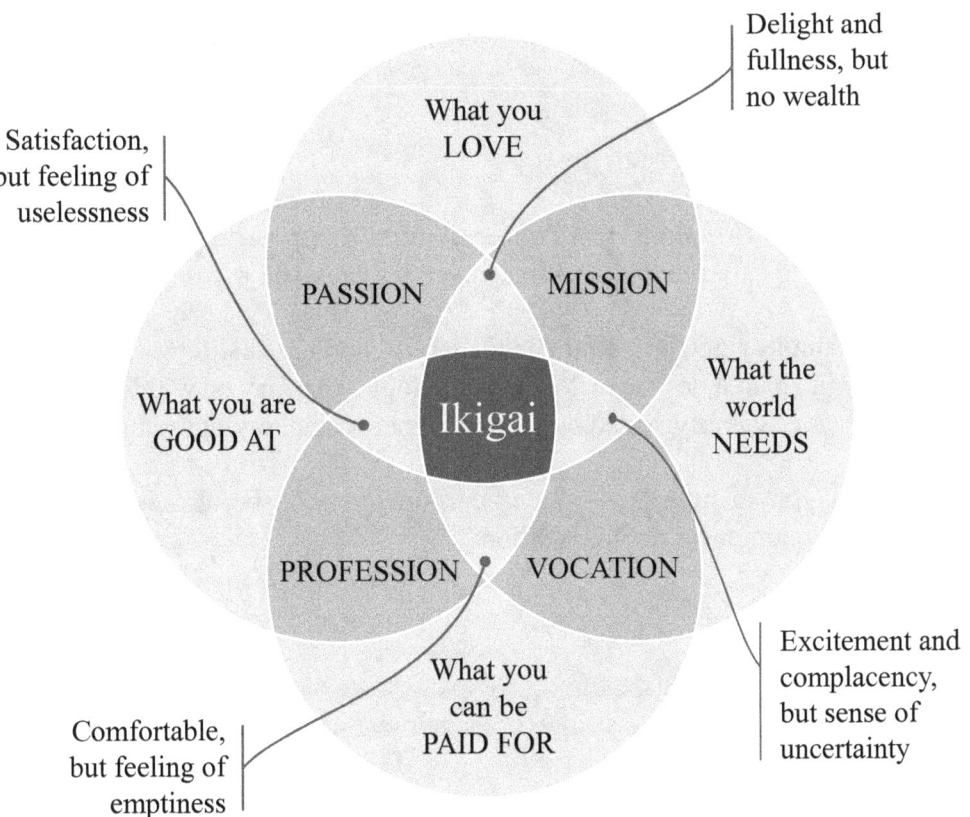

Ikigai is a Japanese concept meaning "a reason for being".

Journal Reflection Questions:

- What do I love?
- What do I care about?
- What does the world need?
- What can I be paid for?

Stretching the Imagination

Right now, you are the creator and designer of your life. What's before you is a blank canvas. You can decide whatever you want. You are only limited by your imagination. You have unlimited wishes.

What do you want?

What are your biggest desires?

What is the first thing that comes to mind that you think would be amazing to experience? (That may even frighten you a little bit).

For example, right now, your goal may be to purchase a three-bedroom house in an area deemed affordable. By logic, this may be within your realm of possibility, based on your current income, savings plan etc.

I want you to make that three-bedroom house a brand new five-bedroom home in a dream location.

How does this feel?

Is your first thought to think, "No way, there is no way this could happen"? Or was there a tinge of excitement and a "what if" kind of feeling?

If the "what if" came a little too easily, where could you expand the vision? To really challenge your thoughts of what is possible?

Imagine owning two luxury homes. Or make them even bigger until you hit your ceiling of possibility, that there is just no way that it is ever going to happen.

The objective of this exercise is to stretch you to a place in which you thought, "No, this would never happen".

We all have this ceiling of belief, and unfortunately for some, the ceiling is very low.

When designing the life you desire, it is important to know what to do when doubt or the thought of impossibility creeps in. It is simply to take that leap of faith forward into the belief of possibility, minus any evidence or logic.

Despite everything else, accept that it is possible.

Scripting the life you want

> *"Imagination is everything. It is the preview to life's coming attractions"*
>
> ~Albert Einstein

An interesting exercise in understanding how much you actually limit yourself is to undertake an exercise of scripting the life you want – ultimately creating a shopping list.

In your journal, start making a list of all things you want in every area of your life. There is no limit, and everything is possible. Notice where you limit or second-guess yourself. The goal is to script the life you want. Observe where you hold yourself back and note what thoughts and corresponding emotions come up.

The purpose of this exercise is to stretch your mind, to create an opening beyond your current limitations. You want to repeat this exercise until it feels easy and comfortable.

One way that you can approach is the Be, Do, Have exercise.

Who would you like to be?

What would you like to do?

What would you like to have?

To escalate this exercise to the next level, I highly recommend adding images. The vision boarding process has been outlined in the Tools and Resources chapter.

Higher and Lower Self

There are two versions in which we show up. At our best, we are patient, loving, kind, courageous, forgiving, curious, and empathetic to the needs of others.

We have an attitude of learning and growth.

In our highest and best version of being, we value the self, know our worth, and contribute to life and others. This is referred to as the higher self.

Showing up as your highest self means operating and living life in communication with a higher level of consciousness, without the restraints of limiting beliefs.

And then there is the other side of the coin. In this state, we are emotionally reactive, stagnated, closed off to any new information, argumentative and operating in victim mode. This is a contracted and closed off energy space. This is referred to as the lower self.

> *"Feeling sorry for yourself and your present condition is not only a waste of energy but the worst habit you could possibly have."*
>
> ~ Dale Carnegie

Operating in our highest and best self means we are in an open and expansive state. Our source of power is to tap into higher energetic frequencies, healing, wisdom, insight, and intuition.

This is where our true power lies and where we want to play – where we positively create and influence the world around us. Contracted energy is also an energy of creation. However, it is the manifestation of all the things we don't want.

The good news is that we get to decide which version of ourselves we show up as. This is called free will.

It can be debated as free will because we may have been operating in a particular way, as a specific version of ourselves for so long, that it feels ingrained as part of our identity and who we are, and therefore deemed as beyond our control.

Without a shadow of a doubt, it has been proven that who we identify with is a self-fulfilling prophecy. Therefore it makes perfect sense to upgrade our identity to match the life and results we want.

To create a new identity, you need to let go of who you think you are – your lower self – to discover the best and highest version of yourself.

There will be resistance to letting go of who you think you are. Because the story is deeply ingrained in your identity, and if you were not that anymore, who would you be?

It is hard to believe that a person would be reluctant to let go of something that gives them so much pain, even if it is for something better, but this is how it is. This is a victim mentality with a purpose.

For example, a person who has been emotionally affected by abandonment at a young age will often experience relationships resulting in further abandonment because a big part of their identity is being an abandoned child.

This is further cemented by the stories they tell themselves (and anyone who will listen) about the situation. Their thoughts and behaviour (driven by this past event) include consciously and unconsciously pushing people away to further reinforce the abandonment story.

A new identity starts by dropping the stories and narrative that keep us chained to the past and operating in the lowest version of ourselves.

The World is Your Mirror

"When the voice and the vision on the inside is more profound and more clear and loud than all opinions on the outside, you've begun to master your life."

~ Dr John Demartini

One of the most challenging concepts for people to accept (including those deep into this practice!) is that the world around us reflects our inner world.

The relationships, the bank balance, the number on the scales, the environment (be it toxic or healthy), the experiences – is a reflection and mirror of what is happening within.

This is a big, and at times, quite an uncomfortable truth to be reminded of. Yet, it is liberating in the sense of recognising what it reveals about ourselves. Even better is that the solution to changing all of it for the better is within us.

For example, if you feel a person or an environment is toxic, the healthy self-reflection questions would be to ask:

How and where am I thinking or behaving in a toxic manner?

What is this situation showing me about myself?

What is bothering me so much about this person or situation?

Rather than looking at what is happening externally, start listening closely to your words and inner dialogue. This will reveal the lens through which you see and experience the world.

Your Problem is Your Problem

Often, we will blame another person for holding us back, or feel angry with them that they are not supporting us, or criticising our dreams and actions. What is important to remember is that if you have a problem with another person, then the problem belongs to you.

It's not their voice that you don't like. It's *your voice* that you don't like.

When you resolve within yourself what you don't like about what you think they are saying, the problem will disappear. You simply won't attract it anymore, or else what they are saying will just slide off you: it won't hit any part of you inside.

A helpful process to understand what this person that you are labelling as the problem, is showing you. When that other person is like a puppet in your head, telling you off, criticising you, or when you are angry with them for being a hypocrite or judgemental. Write down absolutely every single thing you hear them saying, the emotion you are feeling, how it makes you feel about them.

And then read back over all of it and just replace their name with your own.

It's a very enlightening process.

It can be easier to blame someone else than it is to take responsibility that it is our own negative belief system, and lack of faith in ourselves, that is keeping us stuck.

The Power of Your Words

At the core of meditation scripts, affirmations, mantras, and prayers are a specific language that focuses your energy and thoughts towards what you want.

Our words breathe life into our desires.

For example, it is not surprising to hear someone in a world of struggle respond with what they do not want when asked what they do want.

Our words reaffirm our thoughts and beliefs.

The person constantly mentioning that they are tired, broke, feeling angry, sick, in pain or blaming, literally continues to speak into existence all of the things they say they do not want.

However, when the person's language is a consistent affirmation of their wealth, health and gratitude, they are speaking into existence this reality.

Our words set the goal. It is from here that our subconscious mind will get the goal.

Expanding your vocabulary to expand your world

Expanding our vocabulary does more than improving our reading and writing skills. It expands our ability to communicate and up-levels our thinking.

Limited vocabulary can box us in with how we see things. For example, it was interesting for me to note how much I used the words **right** or **wrong** in general discussions or when reflecting.

The drawback with using these words is that they are accompanied by a lot of judgement towards self, others or a situation, leaving very little room for understanding or forgiveness. Whereas when I made a conscious effort to replace them or remove them from a discussion, it changed the course and energy of the conversation.

Questions are the Answers

There is a common saying that there is no such thing as a dumb question. This is not entirely true. Because when it comes to the power of our thoughts and mind, there are *self-destructive* questions.

When you consider the conscious mind as the goal "setter" (done through the thoughts we think and the words we speak), and our subconscious mind the goal "getter" (serving us up the answers through these directions), you can see how questions such as *"why do these things always happen to me?"* after a negative experience can be a self-destructive question.

When you think about it, there are no positive responses to that question.

When you speak those words, you are potentially going to get responses like:

- Because I am stupid
- Because I deserve it
- Because I'm unlucky
- Because it's always been this way

Very few people will ever have a positive response to this line of questioning. Examples of powerful question which speak to and seek a solution are:

- What do I need to learn or do differently to avoid this next time?
- What is my lesson here?
- What is good about this situation?
- How can I turn this into a win or an opportunity?

When you ask better questions, you get better answers. When you ask powerful questions, you get life-changing results.

The secret to asking better questions is to stop speaking and start listening more.

Flipping the Script

Speaking of what you don't want has the stigma of being wrong or bad. When in fact, it can be seen as a contrast and a reveal of an internal avoidance. The language of what I don't want becomes a problem when it stops there, with no communication of what you do want.

This process is about acknowledging what you don't want: using it as the contrast to expand your awareness to what you want, and then speaking that into existence.

The word "should" reveals to us an activity or an action that we know we need to take. Yet, we are avoiding it because the carrot, stick or motivation is not big enough to inspire us into action. Interestingly enough, the "should" statements eventually turn into "I have to" statements.

For example, *"I should do my taxes"* becomes *"I have to do my taxes".* *"I should do some exercise"* becomes *"I have to exercise".*

Remember, taking note of and recognising your language is not about wrong or right. It is about recognising what your words reveal to you.

> *"When you change the way you look at things, the things you look at change."*
>
> ~ Wayne Dyer

Shift Your Gaze

Shifting your gaze is the practice of changing your perspective of a situation, which changes the story you tell yourself and others.

Shifting your gaze is learning how to reframe what you are currently seeing or experiencing. To come at it from another angle than how you are presently conditioned to see things.

When you change perspective, you change the story, and you will change your life.

It is as simple as dropping a narrative and replacing it with a new narrative that is not justified or linked to the old one.

My strongest memory of an example is, from the moment I decided to stop drinking, my story was "I don't drink". I was adamant about not labelling myself as an alcoholic.

Drinking was in the past and had no place in my present. My purpose was clear – stop drinking, start meditating.

I do not drink – this was my new identity.

From the day I decided to stop drinking, I followed it up with a new narrative to reinforce my identity. Through my decision and my new identity, the temptation of drinking was never an option.

Whereas I had a wishy-washy decision to step up and be the person to write this book. I had a story that I kept repeating: "I am almost there, not quite, just need to do some more mindset work".

This was my story for two years and as a consequence, I did not start writing for two years. Even after I started writing the book, this story still continued. Until it came to a day when I was asked – are you there or are you not?

"Almost there" is no closer to "there" than I was two years ago. All it took was a moment to sit with which identity I wanted to own.

Did I want to be the person who stepped into writing this book, or be the person who was almost there?

Athletes don't diet. They train and eat to fuel their body.

Who you identify as, dictates what you do.

The Thing is Never The Thing

The thing we think is the thing is never the thing.

Think about a time in your life when you had a problem, a challenge or struggled with something. You will often look at "the thing" as being the problem.

But when we think about the thing as not being the thing, what it helps us do is see that thing for what it really is.

The thing we think is the thing – the effect – is simply an outward or physical representation of a belief system. It is this which is the real thing that we need to address – the cause.

When we focus on the effect, all we are doing is moving our attention away from resolving the root cause of the problem. We get stuck in a never ending looping cycle.

It is easy and self-deceptive to blame a thing or another for being the problem. For example, alcohol is the problem. *"If I get rid of alcohol, I get rid of the problem"*, or *"my boss is the problem. If I had a better boss, things at work would be so much better".*

The problem with this is that it distracts us from seeing where the real issue and root causes are; which, in turn, results in seeking a short term band-aid solution.

Additionally, this focuses our energy and attention on what we don't want. For example, the problem is that you are broke: *"I've got no money"*. You believe the solution to be that if you had more money, this problem would go away.

We hustle and focus on making more money to fix the current issue of a lack of funds. Or we bury our heads in the sand. Ignoring and being unaware of the underlying problem of not feeling worthy, having poor cash flow management, or taking inconsistent action adds to the problem.

Ignoring the repeating cycle of no-money-to-hustle-to-no-money – the feast or famine cycle – often leads to more problematic behaviours and situations.

The moment you notice yourself pointing the finger of blame and defining something as a problem, remind yourself that the thing is never the thing. Look within to see where you are contributing or creating the current situation.

What can you do differently?

Going back to the above examples:

Problematic drinking

The old way of thinking: if I stop drinking, everything will get better.

A new way of thinking: what is alcohol giving me or helping me to avoid, and what is a healthier and more empowering way to solve this problem?

Who do I need to be, and how do I have to show up to not have this problem?

My boss makes my life hard.

The old way of thinking: if I had a better boss or a different job, everything would be perfect.

The Happiness Hunter's Creed

While the creed is our code of conduct as a collective, ultimately and foremost, it is how we show up each day and operate as individuals.

We are Leaders

I take 100% responsibility for my results and outcomes. I know that true leadership starts with self. I am self aware and walk with integrity.

We are Decisive

I am focused - I make decisions and commit to the outcome by following through. I know that the decisions I make today shape my future. I trust that when I make a decision, everything falls into place to make it happen.

We are Courageous

I am brave and I step into fear. I embrace and celebrate emotional triggers in my life as opportunities to uncover and strengthen my weaknesses. I am resilient.

We are Grateful

I recognise and appreciate the value in all that is before, within and to be. I generously and freely express my gratitude daily. I actively seek out the miracles and joy in every moment.

We are Forgiving

I am compassionate. I know that I am going to make mistakes, and that this is how I learn and grow. I am loving.

We Show Up

I show up for me, especially when I don't want to, and things feel really hard. I am committed to my growth and results. I know who I am, and my identity and values align with my goals and vision.

We Take Action

I am focused and action oriented - recognising the force and the power of a clear focus and positive action. I live my life in the field of play. I play all out.

We are Flexible

If something is not working, I adjust according to the feedback. I have a growth mindset. I am open to new ideas and different ways of doing things.

We are Solution Focused

I look for the gift and learning in all situations. I pause and review the data, and ignore the drama. I take the lessons from the past, live in the now and build for the future.

We have Fun

I know how to laugh at myself and without taking myself too seriously. If I see someone without a smile, I give them one of mine. I play, because it keeps me young.

We are Community

I am a part of something that is bigger than me - the sum of the whole is greater than the individual parts. I treat myself with love, respect and integrity and extend this to others. I know that I am not alone, and that I am always supported.

A new way of thinking: what am I doing to contribute to this difficulty in our relationship?

"What am I seeing in this person that I don't like, and how may I be doing this myself?" (the world is our mirror).

Remember that all problems can be resolved, and the solution starts with present moment awareness.

Your Code of Conduct

Large organisations have vision and mission statements to remind the public and staff about their operating principles and values.

Sports teams, schools and religious groups have a code of conduct as their reference point.

The purpose of these creeds and mission statements, is to remind the groups members and associates of the standard and guiding principles of how they show up. A vision and identity aligned with the best version of self.

It makes perfect sense for us to have our own.

The Happiness Hunter's Intention, shown below, is a reminder of the mission and the space created for community members.

> *May this be a space for connection to our heart;*
> *for unconditional love, happiness, kindness,*
> *acceptance, forgiveness, compassion and*
> *peace – for ourselves, each other*
> *and for the world.*

The Happiness Hunter's Creed, is a reminder of how we show up as our best and highest version – individually and collectively.

The power of this is being able to refer to it when feeling stuck, or "*less than*", and asking yourself as you work through each point: "*am I being this?*"

When I step into my vision as the best version of myself, the creed above is how I think and operate. There are days where we can forget to check-in, or perform and show up at less than ideal energy or attitude. By reading, connecting and reminding myself of this creed, I instantly lift the standard of how I show up.

And on those days and times when I feel any resistance, I re-write the creed into my journal (by hand), read it out loud, and repeat until I feel myself wholly embracing it.

Letting Go of Old Belief Systems and Stories

Some stories are easy to let go of – a simple matter of recognising the benefits and consequences of what it holds for us.

Then there are the stories that need guidance and support to see it from a different perspective to reframe or let go.

Often, this requires us to look at a situation or an event from another person's perspective, not just from our own perspective.

For example, if there was an argument between three friends. At this moment, your recollection of the event is your version, a perspective derived from your personal and emotional experience.

This means revisiting this event and seeing it from each person's view, understanding what they wanted to communicate, how they might have felt, and what they may have seen.

For this to work, you need to separate from any emotion, judgement or bias to the situation. What it does is create empathy and dissolves the emotional attachment we have.

We want to remind ourselves that the human experience is universal.

At times, we are all just simply muddling our way through.

We all make decisions, say things, and behave in a certain way based on how we are feeling at that moment. When we see things from another person's perspective, to understand what may have been going on for them at the time, we step into the position of having powerful and empowered relationships and learn to let go of past hurts and resentments.

Acknowledging our Thoughts

One of the greatest misconceptions of deciding to live a solution-focused and happy life is dismissing our internal self-talk and thoughts without acknowledging and unpacking them.

"Just think positive thoughts" or *"cut the cords of attachment"* are half-baked solutions that do not address what is actually going on.

Our thoughts and internal dialogue are trying to tell us something. Because it may be something that doesn't feel good at that moment or triggers uncomfortable emotions, it is easy to dismiss them. When in fact, you are ignoring and burying the message.

Just think about what happens to the nagging parent when we ignore them. Their voice gets louder until, eventually, it becomes a physical discomfort. On the flip side, what happens when we respond and engage with the parent's request – the nagging stops. The same can be said for what happens between our ears.

For those who embrace a connection to a higher source of wisdom, it is easy then to see that the internal communication dialogue is presented in a way for us to take notice.

Next time you catch a looping thought or self-talk that feels uncomfortable, take a moment to acknowledge it.

Ask yourself, "What is the message here?" and "What is this thought and what do my feelings about it show me – what is it that I may need to acknowledge, learn or release?"

Continue to ask questions until you come up with two to three positive action-based solutions. Journalling is also a great practice to help with this. Should the thought come up again, repeat the process.

> *"What we resist persists."*
> ~ Carl Jung

It is also worth noting that the answer may not present itself immediately when you ask the questions above. Trust, know that you have set the thought path in motion, and the answer will eventually reveal itself.

Be open to where and how the answer may come.

Making Miracles Happen

Faith is a miracle activator.

Miracles come in many forms and are all around us. A walk in the park and we are surrounded by the miracle of nature in the plants, the miracle of the bee and the continuation of life through the miracle of pollination, the miracle of trees converting carbon dioxide to oxygen, providing shade, shelter and food.

Take a moment to think about how you are made up at the biological level – our bodies' ability to regenerate cells and heal itself. The ability to think and to have conscious self-awareness is one of the greatest miracles. The brain is a miracle supercomputer. And let's not forget the miracle of conception to birth.

These and so much more are miracles of life. We are surrounded by miracles, and they will continue to happen – whether you notice them or not.

Then there are the miracles that we activate through a conscious decision to believe.

Transformation happens through a series of consistent actions. This is true for both the desired and undesired transformation.

In transformation, we have two choices. We can achieve results through action, or we can experience an extraordinary outcome beyond our imagination when we couple action with faith within and with a higher power.

Extraordinary transformation and results are achieved with the formula of attitude plus action plus faith.

A miracle is a life in action and extraordinary events called forward through faith.

"Miracles, in the sense of phenomena we cannot explain, surround us on every hand: life itself is the miracle of miracles."

~ George Bernard Shaw

Faith in a Higher Power

As a note here, when I first decided to choose happiness, God/a higher power/spirituality was not part of this equation. I just wanted to be happy. It was a surprising and very unexpected gift to experience this connection. Awareness of and desire for this connection now underpins every aspect of my life.

This is not something I would have believed back in 2012.

I am not here to tell you what you should or should not believe. But it would be remiss of me not to share the profound impact this growing relationship has had for me. Leaning into that unconditional love and support is so much of who I am and how I got to where I am today. I know that I am never on my own.

Our spiritual connection is a deeply personal thing. It is equally accessible for all of us when we are ready. Just know that whatever your current belief is – the information shared in this book does not rely on your belief in God to be valid.

And for the record. In my experience, meditation is the key to opening the door to this connection.

> "Even though I walk through the darkest valley, I will fear no evil, for you are with me; your rod and your staff, they comfort me."
>
> ~ Psalm 23:4

In Greek, the word for faith is "pistis", which means "the act of giving one's trust".

There are two types of faith. The first is faith in self. In action, this means having confidence in one's ability to achieve what you have set out to do, despite any evidence or limiting beliefs to the contrary.

Then there is faith in a force beyond ourselves. For me, I know this as God. You may call it your higher self, the universe, source, creator or spirit. Just know this, whatever you call it, it plays the exact role of a higher power at play for all of us.

Faith is often one of the first casualties when we are hit with a significant crisis or setback in life. Loss of faith presents as self-doubt. When we lose faith, we start to doubt, which feeds any limiting beliefs or stories we may have. This in turn manifests as a repeating pattern, habit, or event in our life.

Regaining faith is the simple act of looking for and acknowledging the miracles in your life.

A magical thing happens when we start seeing and appreciating the miracles: the more you see, the more miracles happen to and for us.

Make miracles a regular part of your day.

How Does a Miracle Happen?

> *"What lies before us and what lies behind us, are but small matters compared to what lies within us."*
> ~ Henry Haskins

Activating a miracle requires acts of faith. There will be many situations where it will be challenged, and self-doubt will kick in. This is where leaning into the faith that everything is working out perfectly for you will take effect.

The deeper I lean into the truth of who I am, the richer my life experience is becoming.

When you get some news that doesn't go your way or isn't what you wanted to hear:

- The first step is to pause (not react), acknowledge, name and feel the emotion.

- Notice any story that you start to tell yourself as a result of this situation.

- Notice if it feeds self-doubt or a lack of self-worth, and then course-correct with a simple affirmation:

> *"This may not be what I wanted, but I have faith that it is absolutely what I need because I know that I am always looked after."*

- Keep repeating it until you emotionally connect with it.

Ask, Believe and Receive

"We are divine enough to ask, and we are important enough to receive."
~ Wayne Dyer

ASK

Asking is the act of communicating what we want.

We have all heard of the warning, be careful what you wish for, so it becomes imperative to be aware of how you may be asking for things you don't want. This often happens through a lack of clarity about knowing what you do want. Get clarity first, then create a clear, concise sentence asking for what you want.

I ask, fearlessly and with conviction, for what I truly want.

Affirmation: *For this or better, for the highest good of all concerned. And so it is done.*

"One of life's fundamental truths states, 'Ask and you shall receive'. As kids, we get used to asking for things, but somehow we lose this ability in adulthood. We come up with all sorts of excuses and reasons to avoid any possibility of criticism or rejection."
~ Jack Canfield

BELIEVE

Belief is the act of holding something true. We have beliefs that serve us and those that hold us back in our growth – often referred to as limiting beliefs. There is a funny thing about beliefs because often they are backed by misconstrued evidence, none of which would stand up in a court of law.

Beliefs are formed in defining moments, where a suggestion or opinion is presented by another or through an event. What we do at that moment is mentally and often unconsciously try that opinion on for size.

If it fits, we own it, even when it is unhealthy or a derogatory belief. We then continue to validate it with supporting evidence, not letting the truth get in the way of our story.

Our beliefs are closely tied to our identity. The stronger we feel about our identities emotionally, the harder we will fight to hold onto that belief and continue to tell the stories to support it.

If you believe, anything is possible.

This is why you will hear: *change your story, change your life, and decide who you need to be in your highest and best version to achieve what you want to achieve.*

RECEIVE

"Everything comes to us that belongs to us if we create the capacity to receive it."
~ Rabindranath Tagore

There are no boundaries or limits to abundance, success and prosperity. This is a universal truth.

Most of us misunderstand this universal truth by believing that we need to create the object, event or person of our desire. When the truth of the matter is, once we have conceived it, it already exists. We are only limited by how much we allow ourselves to receive.

To receive well, we need to first recognise where we are rejecting what we desire.

We reject through disbelief, doubt and lack of worth. This is often presented as self-sabotage. We reject when we focus on what we don't want. Remember, the energy flows where our attention goes.

We reject through a lack of acknowledgement. How often have you rejected a compliment or dismissed a small accomplishment?

How to receive

In recognition of a compliment, result or win, no matter what size, take a moment to recognise how you respond.

Do you ignore it?

Is your self-talk dismissive, or down-plays the win by referencing it as "luck"?

If so, you are actively rejecting abundance, and often what you reject is the very thing you desire.

To course-correct this, pause, acknowledge the compliment or win by repeating it to yourself and say:

Thank you, I receive this with love and grace.

The Seven Elements

"The key is taking responsibility and initiative, deciding what your life is about and prioritising your life around the most important things."

~ Stephen Covey

Happiness Quotient

The Happiness Quotient (HQ) is a basic tool designed to help you understand how you **think and feel** about where you are across each area of your life.

It developed from an idea and concept back in 2013, where I got together with an old work colleague and friend, Paul O'Brien. Over a coffee, we scratched out and expanded on an idea which became The Seven Elements – A Framework for Life Integration.

From there, we both continued to teach and coach clients through this framework. It has evolved to match our individual message and style.

Life Integration

Everything you do is part of your life, even work.

Life Integration is about seeking balance across all areas of your life – recognising that everything in your life and that everything you do is inextricably linked.

Understanding that when one or two (or three or four…) elements are out of whack will impact the other areas and, therefore, the quality of your life.

It is about giving you permission to get clear on a happy, healthy, abundant, successful, loving life and what it means for you. As well as giving you permission to start living that life today.

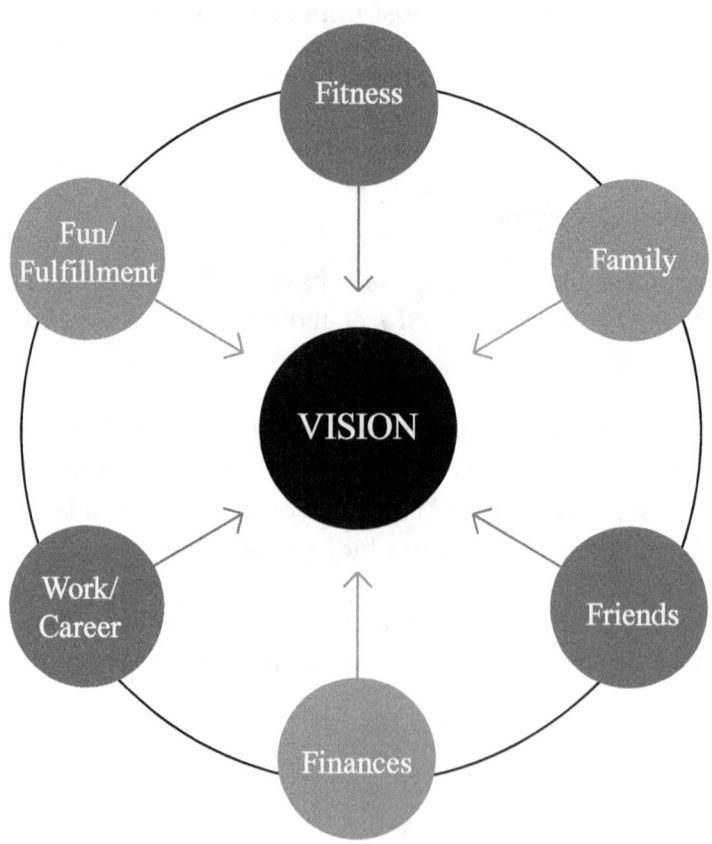

SUCCESSFUL LIFE INTEGRATION CAN BE ACHIEVED WHEN YOU:

- Have a clear vision for what a successful life means for you
- Have a clearly defined decision-making framework
- Understand your priorities and what is important
- Have clarity on your goals
- Have an action plan, with built in accountability mechanisms
- Take complete responsibility for your life, your mindset and your emotions
- Know when things are out of balance within any element of your life or across The Seven Elements
- Give yourself permission to do what is important to maintain and regain balance
- Accept that you are the only person who can change things

WHAT ARE THE SEVEN ELEMENTS?

Vision
Developing a concrete picture of who you want to be in your life and how you want to be living it, getting clear on your motivating drivers, desired lifestyle and core values.

Fitness
You are the most important element in your life. Getting clarity on your desired state of wellbeing – physically, mentally, spiritually, emotionally.

Family
Getting clear on the types of relationships you would like to have with your intimate and extended family and what that means for how you show up in your role in each of these relationships.

Friends

Creating and maintaining connections with those you trust – and broader community and support networks – who enrich your life, keep you honest and offer unconditional support, including emotionally.

Finances

Making financial security and a positive relationship with money an essential part of your life.

Work/Career

Identifying your passion and work goals in light of other critical elements in your life.

Fun/Fulfilment

Expansion and growth – reintegrating those things (hobbies, leisure, volunteering, community, sport etc.) that can drop away when you become overwhelmed by daily activities. Giving yourself permission to have fun, relax and enjoy your life.

My Happiness Quotient

The purpose of this activity is to help give you an overview of how well-balanced you think or feel your life is at the moment – it is a baseline for where you are now. It is not a scientific test, nor are there any right or wrong answers.

It will simply shine a spotlight on which elements you think or feel are going well and where there is room for improvement.

Once you have completed it, you will have clarity about your priorities to move forward in the desired direction. Some of the gaps will have possible actions you can take that will be straightforward (for example, do more exercise and go for a walk). Still, some may reveal deeper causes and need a strategic approach (for example, relationship issues or overcoming money blocks).

HQ Self-Assessment

VISION – who and how you want to be in your life
How happy are you with the direction of your life?

FITNESS – physical, mental, emotional, social and spiritual wellbeing
How happy do you feel with your overall health, fitness and wellbeing?

FAMILY – the relationships you have with those closest to you
How do you rate the health and happiness of your intimate and extended family relationships?

FRIENDS – the relationships of choice
How fulfilled and nourished are you with your social support and broader networks?

FINANCES – creating financial security
How secure do you feel with your financial situation, and your relationship with money?

WORK/CAREER – the thing you do to generate money
How happy are you with your work, environment and contribution?

FUN AND FULFILLMENT – what expands, fulfills and grows us
How happy are you with the amount of time you spend on additional activities (i.e. community work, volunteering, having fun, hobbies, travel, projects etc.)? Is it quality time?

There will most likely be common themes showing up for you throughout the process. Some of these may be due to your perception, which can be shifted in an instant – a quick gratitude practice will help do this.

Remember, you experience the world as YOU see it, and how you see it is due to your beliefs, self-talk, memories and experience.

REMEMBER, If you are not happy, you can choose to change.

It is that simple.

Journal Activity

In your journal, draw a line down the page to create a column. Column one on the left is where you currently are. Column two is where you want to be.

Under the heading of each element in column one:

- On a scale of one to 10, with one being very unhappy and 10 being extremely happy, rate your feeling for each statement.
- Make a list and note the thoughts, behaviours and actions of self that are holding you back.

In the second column (the right-hand column), under the heading of each element:

- On a scale of one to 10, rate where you want to be.
- Make a list of the new thoughts, behaviours, activities, tools, resources and knowledge.
- Include and write down any thoughts that present themselves.

Do not overthink the process, just go with what comes first. Be honest.

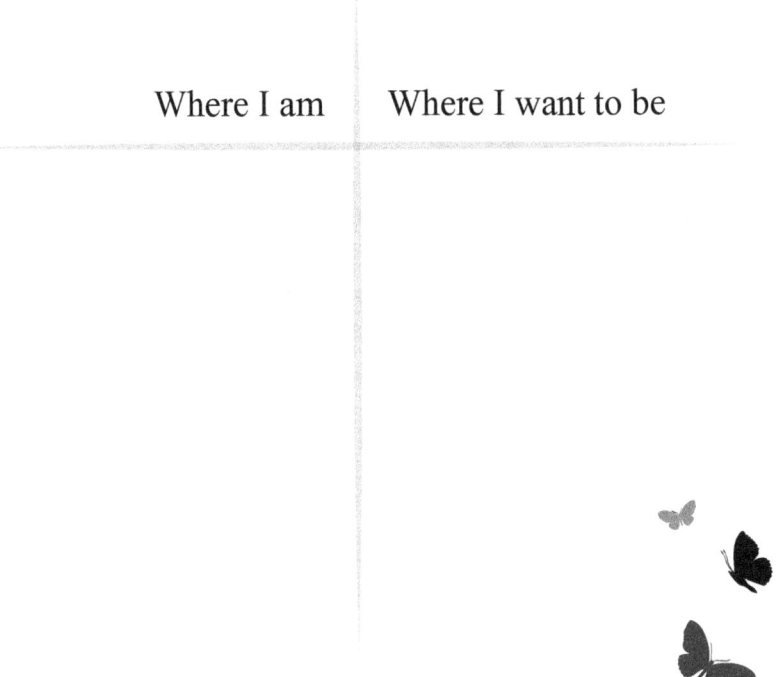

Gaps and Priorities

Now it is time to understand the gaps between where you are now and where you would like to be. Look at the column on the left – where you are actually at – and note the difference in how it feels in relation to where you would like to be in the column on the right: where you would like to be.

A gap is a thought, action or behaviour that you need to either stop or start doing to get what you want.

Example One:

In column one (where you currently are), you may carry more weight than healthy, i.e. 30kgs overweight.

In column two (where you want to be), you are at your ideal weight.

The gap here is 30kgs (needs to be eliminated).

Example Two:

In column one (where you currently are), you may binge watch television with one to two sessions a week of exercise.

In column two (where you want to be), you exercise for 60 minutes – four to five times a week.

The gap between what is missing and what needs to be eliminated is to reduce the amount of television watched (reduced/eliminated) and increasing exercise (new activity/practice).

Whatever you have in the left-hand column, make sure that there is a corresponding and tangible action or outcome in the right-hand column.

Now, write a list of all the actions against each outcome in the right-hand side column.

Prioritising and Quick Wins

There are two steps in this next section. The first is to highlight and understand any quick wins. The second being to do the same with activities and actions that need a little more strategy, effort and action behind them.

Step One :
Review your action list and highlight any quick wins that can be quickly addressed and implemented (e.g. drink more water, turn off the television). Park these for the next step of the exercise.

Step Two:
With the remaining action items, list them in the order of priority, starting with number one as the most important action, which, if implemented, would have the most significant influence and impact on results.

Your complete action list includes all of the elements. Choose your top three to begin the goal setting and planning process.

Journal Reflection Questions

In your journal, reflect on these questions for The Seven Elements HQ exercise, once again making a note of any other thoughts that come up.

- How did it make you feel as you were completing the HQ?
- How do you feel now?
- The five things that I love the most about my life right now are...

Drivers, Values and Vision

"Goals help you channel your energy into action."

~ Les Brown

There are many elements at play when it comes to setting and achieving goals successfully.

First of all, there is the strategic plan.

Add to this the attitude and mindset of knowing your drivers, values and vision.

Additionally, having the behavioural flexibility to assess your results along the way and adjust accordingly.

And finally, having a non-negotiable commitment to consistent action and follow through with your plan.

Understanding the Journey – The Messy Middle

Goals are exciting at the beginning, a celebration at the end, and a lot of mess in the middle.

Knowing and accepting that the journey of getting from where you are to where you want to be may not always be a smooth ride (in fact, at times, it may be very far from pretty). This IS the process of achieving any worthwhile goal.

Many misunderstand and forget that it is so much more than just about the outcome that has cause for celebration, the real magic and value is in the person you become during the process.

Drivers, Values and Vision

Understand what your drivers, values and vision are, and you will understand your decision-making process. The advantage of knowing your decision-making framework is that if it is not working, you can edit and adjust.

For example, suppose you find you are making decisions that work against your goals. In that case, you can edit and adjust any one of them to set yourself up for success.

The non-negotiable decision-making framework comprises three pillars. Understanding your drivers, values, and vision will provide you with your why.

It is Possible

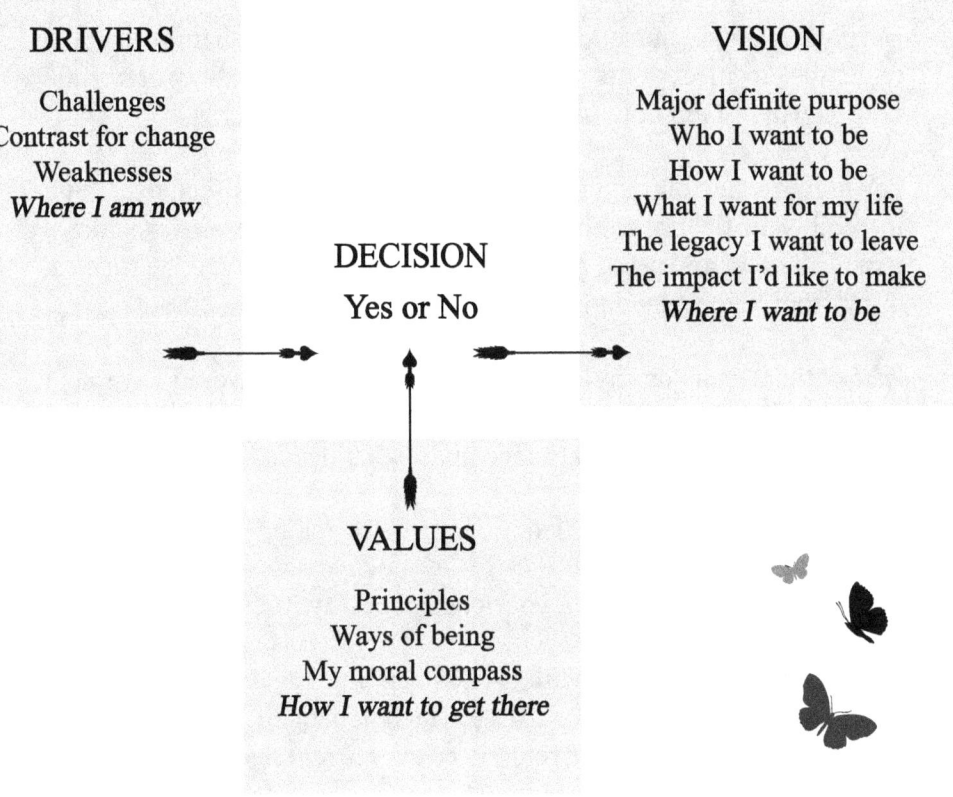

DRIVERS

Your driving motivation forms one of the three pillars, and it is often this awareness that keeps us going through the darkest of times.

In its simplest form, driving motivators include what we don't want and are often the contrast for what we want to change.

- Why are you here?
- Why do you want to change?
- What do you want to change?
- What is the issue that is causing the biggest problem for you?
- What are your catalysts for change?

Be honest with yourself. There is nothing to be ashamed of, and remember to meet yourself with love and compassion – *where I am now, is where I am now, and where I am now is perfect.*

For me, my starting point was being deeply, deeply unhappy. Being incredibly unfit, unhealthy, drinking way too much, feeling like a terrible mother and being in a relationship that I considered the furthest thing from being fun (and that's putting it mildly).

Rather than focus on my current experience (which would have kept me stuck in more of the same), I decided to focus on what I wanted instead. But first, I needed to face up to what needed to change.

I needed to eyeball it. I needed to describe my pain.

Step One is to take a look at your current reality.

I was reminded of this while I was reading my first goal setting statement from the start of 2012, which I happened to find while moving house in 2021. I had referenced my current reality of the things I didn't like and no longer wanted.

The following text is my actual written goal statement:

> *"I have been drinking a ridiculous amount of alcohol and started smoking again, which makes me wake up at 3am in the morning full of self-loathing.*
>
> *I can't be bothered parenting when I am tired and hungover. I don't like myself very much at the moment.*
>
> *My cholesterol is at the high end of normal, and my doctor has told me I need to lose weight. I can feel my fat wobble, my back is constantly sore, my thighs rub together, I can't handle the heat, my clothes don't fit. I don't like getting into bathers or even tight-fitting exercise pants."*

You will notice that my language is focused on the pain and what I don't want. While this is a great motivator to get started, it's not sustainable to continue to focus on the pain. Look at your goal and make decisive statements as to what you want as well as what you don't want.

Some of my earliest decision statements (drivers) were:

- I never wanted to wake up with a hangover ever again
- I wanted to be an excellent role model for my kids
- I wanted to be the fittest, healthiest and happiest I have ever been

Look at each area within The Seven Elements and in your journal, write three decision statements for each one.

For example, for my health, the three statements were:

- I take care of my body with good nutrition
- I walk every day
- I don't drink alcohol

Review and say them daily.

Values

Values are a person's principles, standards or behaviour, and the moral compass of what is important in life. They are our guiding beacon for happiness and help us to live life well.

Very few of us are really crystal clear on our values.

When we know our values, when we understand why and how they are important, we understand our emotional reactions and decision-making process.

What are Values?

Basic and fundamental beliefs and motivators like integrity, honesty, family, joy, respect and trust guide us in our attitudes and actions.

Values are a way of living, according to our internal code.

Understanding your core value in a particular area (i.e. in a relationship) allows you to compare it against your partner's core value, which in turn opens the discussion as to how they would work together.

For example, one person's value may be freedom in a relationship. The other may have fidelity/loyalty as their core value. This often creates friction in relationships, as most people enter relationships without understanding their core values and how they can work together in harmony.

Freedom in a relationship for most people could be not wanting to be controlled or told what to do. In contrast, it can be perceived as being a lack of commitment to the relationship.

The value question is one to really ponder over and to dig into.

- How do these values apply to different instances?
- What does their practical application actually mean?
- How important is it that other people share a particular value?

What impact would its absence have on your decision-making (for example, being friends with someone or doing business with them)?

You must know yourself well enough to understand what your

boundaries are with regards to your values.

If you look back at an experience in your life that you regret, chances are that it is because it was out of alignment with your values (now you can bring in The Big Guns!)

For each element of your life, list your top five values. For example, the five core top values for a person could be:

Fitness (emotional, physical, mental and spiritual)

1. Spiritual connection
2. Being intentionally active daily
3. Emotional intelligence
4. Nourishing and hydrating my body with quality food
5. Focus

Finances

1. Financial freedom
2. Responsibility
3. Abundance
4. Generosity
5. Trust

Fun and fulfillment

1. Fun
2. Relaxing
3. Personal growth
4. Lifelong learning
5. Creativity

How to Unpack Your Core Values

Step One: Pick one of The Seven Elements and make a list of all the core values important for you.

As a guide, these things would have you with your needs met and feeling fulfilled.

Step Two: Number them in order of priority and importance.

Step Three: Unpack and expand what each value means in an application.

For example, in the Finance example above, freedom was the core value. When queried further and expanded, it evolved into financial freedom when examined. For another, freedom could mean the choice and ability to spend without care or concern.

The top three core values are usually our driving forces.

As an interesting side exercise, reflect on your core values for relationships and then look at a past relationship that didn't work out.

Examples of core values

Creativity	*Compassion*	*Education*
Reliability	*Environmentalism*	*Perseverance*
Loyalty	*Spirit of adventure*	*Fun*
Commitment	*Innovation*	*Service to others*
Open-mindedness	*Positivity*	*Lifelong learning*
Consistency	*Optimism*	*Trust*
Honesty	*Passion*	*Joy*
Efficiency	*Respect*	*Generosity*
Innovation	*Fitness*	
Good humour	*Courage*	

Vision

> *"Vision is the art of seeing what is invisible to others."*
> ~ Jonathan Swift

A vision is a compelling picture or mind movie of the desired reality.

Unfortunately, most of us operate from a vision and mind movie based on our past experiences and limiting beliefs, which ultimately ends up remaining our future.

To create a compelling vision, we need to know what we want and who we want to become. This is why it is crucial to spend time getting clear on what we **really** want.

Without vision, direction and intention, we drift. Sound familiar?

Get clear on who you want to be, how you want to be living and what you want for each element – your highest aspiration.

What we think, we become.

It starts with you

We all want to change and influence our environment, including the people around us, to give ourselves that which we desire (inner peace, love, health, money, relationships etc.).

And we do this by trying to control people and events, not realising that this will give us more of what we don't want.

We don't realise that the biggest impact we can have with getting what we want is how we show up and our level of investment in the process.

If you want love – *start loving you*

If you want peace – *be still*

If you want to be heard – *listen to understand*

If you want to be seen – *see others*

If you want health – *respect, and love yourself enough to be it*

If you want wealth – *see and embrace the abundance around you*

All the things you wish for internally, externally, everything – it starts with you. There is no shortcut. There is no fast-tracking the process. Your journey will be as long as it needs to be until you get it.

> *"You cannot give birth to an adult."*
> ~ Brian Smith

There is a reason as to why all things start within you and your inner world. You don't get what you want. You attract what and who you are.

Putting ourselves first is not selfish

If anything, it is the exact opposite of selfishness. By taking care of ourselves first, we ensure that we can serve and help others from a place of wholeness and abundance of energy and thought.

When we are depleted, we have very little to give. It is in the moments in which we focus and invest in our health, wellbeing and self-care that energises us. We are at our most powerful and magnetic when our cup is full, when we are rested, nourished, balanced and in a growth mindset: this is where the magic happens.

Understanding motivation

There are four overarching drivers in what motivates us. Knowing and understanding them will give you an advantage in how to make them work for you.

Motivation is essentially your reason to act or behave in a particular way, creating a sense of enthusiasm, desire or willingness to do something.

Intrinsic and Extrinsic

Intrinsic is internally motivated behaviour, which is generally driven by an internal reward, for example, being true to your word or a spiritual connection. It is the driving force behind behavioural change.

Intrinsic motivation creates lasting transformation.

The desire to earn or gain physical or material outcomes; for example, money, success, fame or praise, are extrinsic or external motivational forces.

Achieving an external goal can make you feel good on the inside. However, what is important to remember is that motivation started and focused externally does not always last.

When setting your goals, it is worth taking a moment to notice where your motivation driver originates from.

If it is all internally driven, you might want to add some external motivation to give you the best push/pull balance, likewise if your focus is predominantly externally driven. You may want to look at where you can balance it out by introducing and focusing on intrinsic motivational factors.

Having both intrinsically and extrinsically focused motivation will provide you with more push, as well as stacking the odds in your favour.

The push will propel you away from what you don't want, and the pull will draw you towards your goals.

Moving Towards and Moving Away

Language is an excellent indicator of a person's motivation. It reveals if they are moving towards a goal, or away from pain.

For example, if you ask a person why they are on a diet. The one who answers, "I don't want to be fat" moves away from a pain point. The person who answers, "I want to be fit and healthy and at XYZ weight" is desire-driven (moving forward).

Suppose a person is only driven by getting away from a pain point. The likelihood of them giving up once they no longer feel like that and before reaching their goal is high. This is the pattern of a yo-yo dieter or the feast or famine.

On the other end of the spectrum, if a person is only motivated towards a goal, they lack the push of a pain point driver on the days when they are not feeling like showing up.

The point being, is that it is good to have both – a motivation pushing you away from something and a motivator pulling you towards it.

How this would look with someone who wanted to lose weight and get healthy, would be to connect with the pain point of the discomfort of their present circumstances and of not achieving their goals. Couple this with the dream and desire of how they would feel and what they would get when the goal is achieved.

Make sure you have intrinsic, extrinsic, moving away from and towards motivating reasons and drivers.

A word of warning about motivation: it is a feeling, and feelings come and go. Relying on being motivated to do something is putting your goals at the mercy of your environment and feelings – a fluid hit-and-miss strategy.

A better strategy is to have a non-negotiable and consistent action plan with milestones to measure your progress.

Results are what creates motivation. Generate your own motivation and inspiration.

Starting with self is a not-negotiable reference point.

> *Just a heads up!*
>
> *I have found that this is the most challenging step in the process (putting self first) and is the most resisted by those operating with a martyr mindset.*
>
> *Historically, the martyr described a person who was willing to die for their cause. Today, the term* **Martyr Mindset** *is used to describe a person who suffers or self-sacrifices to meet the needs of another or others.*
>
> *The martyr mentality is similar to the victim mentality, however there are some subtle differences. The victim mentality typically feels personally attacked or offended by anything that goes wrong, a mishap or rude behaviour.*
>
> *The martyr mindset tends to "sacrifice" their own needs to get things done for others. Often, what starts as a joyful choice leads to an obligation, which creates internal conflict and resentment.*
>
> *The payoff and benefit for operating from this mindset is the recognition of sacrifice.*
>
> *Experiences may be exaggerated to gain sympathy or hold others as emotional hostages.*
>
> *This happens due to the failure of putting self first.*

Defining Your Not-Negotiables

Look at the daily practices of any successful professional, athlete or master. It will be blindingly obvious that there are sets of practices, habits and routines which are not negotiable.

These are personal contracts, not open to compromise or negotiation. They happen, no matter what.

When I look back at the start of my journey, the things I wanted to do, things I knew would help me and give me what I was seeking – each one of these practices was an option, negotiable (depending on how I felt) and at times, not even on my radar.

As I began to implement new routines and rituals, the results were hit and miss; I got just enough results to know it would work. Still, I was not consistent enough for a complete transformation. Again, it's worth noting that the theme here is that these were negotiable.

When I stepped into the identity of the person who woke up at 5am – waking up at 5am became not-negotiable. It was a part of my identity, and it was who I was.

Not-negotiables start with a decision. That decision is to identify as the person that does (insert practice) without fail because that is who they are.

A Happiness Hunter's Experience

"Today was the first day I woke up early. I went for a walk, meditated, and had showered and gotten ready before my kids woke up. I felt SO MUCH BETTER. I made more progress with my book than I have the past two months, and I made great connections to help build my business. I've been more cheerful and emotionally present with my kids.

One of the things I wrote as a part of my vision is that my kids and I regularly laugh so hard we cry. In just the past two days since I wrote it, it's happened twice. The synchronicity is feeling real.

I'm looking forward to developing my Major Definite Purpose to help clarify my vision and give me greater direction!"

~ Cynthia, The Steps for Change student

Planning for Success

Why Plan for Success?

When we don't take the time to stop and think about where we are and what we want to achieve or how we will get there, we put ourselves into a position where we will find ourselves drifting through life, waiting for things to happen for us. Wondering why we aren't getting anywhere, and why nothing is changing.

Setting goals and creating an action plan is a powerful way to build the life you want.

Setting SMARTER Goals

Setting SMARTER goals means that a goal has been broken down into a process of being: Specific, Measureable, Achievable, Realistic and Timebound. The goal should Excite you enough to motivate you through periods of slumps, and your process should include Review and adjust (if required) and is a proven and Repeatable process.

When goal-setting, it pays to set a single goal for each area of your life. A big one, which, if and when achieved, would have maximum impact and a domino effect in all the other areas.

Start with an area of life, and break it down to meet the SMARTER goal metrics. I've used HEALTH as an example of how to work through this process.

S - Specific

Your goal needs to be specific and concise. Providing a clear vision of what you want to achieve.

Goal: Health

What do I want?
"To be the fittest, healthiest and happiest I've ever been."

What does success look like?
"I want to run a marathon."

Can I be more specific?
"I want to enter and complete a half-marathon."

M - Measurable

Making a goal measurable gives it a metric to create a timeline and milestones. Milestones are the benchmarks along your timeline which let you know whether you are on track or need to adjust.

When do I want to achieve this, or how long will it take?
"I will run the Melbourne half-marathon on (date/month/year)."

What can I measure?
Number of training runs and stretching classes.

Weekly training distance.
Improving running times.

How will I know I achieved it?
"I crossed the finish line."

A - Achievable

When you look at all the metrics of SMARTER goals, specifically concerning time and being measurable – is your goal achievable?

This is a fine line between knowing that it is possible to set your mind to it and set yourself up for success versus setting yourself up for failure.

Is this goal achievable?

"Taking into account my ability, the date of the marathon and my training schedule, is this goal achievable? Yes!"

R - Relevant

Is this goal relevant to improving all other areas of my life and creating the life I desire?

Does this goal align with my core values?

"Yes, my core value is health."

Does this goal align with my vision?

"Yes, my vision is to be the fittest and healthiest person I can be."

Does this goal work in harmony with my other goals?

"Yes, it benefits and moves them along."

T - Timed

The goal can be broken into a timeline with a start, middle and endpoint. It is worth noting that some goals have activities that will continue long after the goal has been met. For example, you may continue running daily after running the marathon.

Is there a start and end date?

"Yes. I start tomorrow, and the marathon is scheduled for (day/month/year)."

Can I schedule the activities to get me to the end goal?

"Yes. I will be running three to five days a week, with strength training and recovery sessions twice a week."

E - Exciting

Your goal should be big enough to scare you a little, yet exciting enough to get you started and keep you going (especially through a slump).

Am I excited about the person I will become when I achieve this goal?

"Yes. I will be a fit, healthy and active marathon runner who trains daily and nourishes my body with good nutrition."

Does this goal challenge me?

"Yes. It is way outside my comfort zone."

Does this goal match my WHY?

"Yes. My 'why' is to be the healthiest and best version of me."

R - Review and Repeat

The best strategy for setting goals is to focus on ones that become a part of the stack of a bigger life vision. For example, running a marathon works towards a bigger goal of leading a healthy and active lifestyle.

Once achieved, the next goal from a marathon could be to enter and complete a triathlon. Both contribute to a healthier lifestyle and create the conditions for growth outside of the comfort zone.

Creating an action plan

Creating an action plan starts with breaking a goal down into milestones. A milestone is a measurable key point of a journey. Not only does this allow you to create a timeline, but it also helps with creating tangible and actionable steps.

So if, for example, your goal was to write a book (this goal focuses on the content creation process), the milestones may look like this:

> *Choose your book topic and subject*
>
> *Map out the chapters, including key points required for each chapter*
>
> *Chapter One (including research)*
>
> *Chapter Two (including research)*
>
> *Chapter Three (including research) etc. until completed*
>
> *Review and edit the first draft*
>
> *Review and edit the second draft*
>
> *External proofread*
>
> *Review and edit*
>
> *Design cover*
>
> *Prepare manuscript for publishing*
>
> *Publish*

Planning the Timeline

First and foremost, be realistic about the required time to achieve your goal in a healthy and sustainable manner. It is easy to get excited when setting a goal and do everything overnight (forgetting all other life responsibilities).

I recommend consistent daily action over an all-or-nothing approach.

In planning the timeline for writing this book, I originally had the ambitious goal below of completing it in 21 weeks.

>Choose book topic and subject – one week.
>
>Map out the chapters and key points – two weeks.
>
>Writing chapters to the first draft – eight weeks.
>
>Review and edit the first draft – four weeks.
>
>Prepare the manuscript for publishing – four weeks.
>
>Publish – two weeks.
>
>Total – 21 weeks.

In reality, it took 24-months. This was a bigger book than my first one and I had underestimated the time needed to review, reflect and edit. A process repeated many times.

The lesson for me in this process was to be flexible with my plan, as I realised my goal was to produce the best book I could, versus the quickest book.

Scheduling

We underestimate the value of scheduling tasks into our calendar. The biggest benefit of scheduling is that it removes the mental clutter of thinking about it by locking in dedicated time to complete the task. Scheduling also allows you to prioritise the important things in your life.

By committing to planning and working your life from a calendar, you have the advantage of foresight to see any upcoming events that may interfere with a writing schedule. For example, my children's school holidays extended a one-week writing schedule of a chapter to two weeks.

An additional advantage was scheduling my writing time around administrative tasks instead of client-facing time. I found this to work best for me.

It always pays to include a healthy buffer of time. Anyone who has been through the writing and publishing process will know that 21-26 weeks is quite an ambitious timeline. Traditional publishing authors are generally given two years to produce a manuscript.

Staying Committed, Motivated and Inspired Action

The truth of the matter is, commitment to your schedule is the only thing that matters. Motivation will come from the results.

Once the initial excitement of starting my second book had worn off, I went through periods where the writing felt like hard work. There were moments where I wasn't sure how it was all going to come together.

By sticking to the plan, I completed more chapters. With each completed chapter, my excitement and motivation increased.

Know, expect and accept that there will be periods of time where you will not be inspired or motivated. In these moments, simply show up and follow the plan – rather than being driven by your emotions.

Self-discipline is following through on your action plans, especially when you don't feel like it.

Reviewing and Assessing

It's worth repeating; the advantage of having milestones and a timeline scheduled into your calendar is a quick snapshot to see how you are tracking. I could see if I was ahead or behind in my writing schedule.

There is a fine line between allowing yourself too much leeway in your schedule, because sometimes a deadline is an excellent stick to make things happen. Yet having a fixed and inflexible mindset will fail to adjust to the ebbs and flows of life.

Suppose I was falling behind with meeting the milestones. In that case, I would check to see if the goal was too ambitious against the milestones and checklist. Or was it simply a case of not following through on the commitment? With this information, I could adjust accordingly.

Building in accountability

Building in external accountability is an excellent supportive motivator to get things done. For example, I shared my goal and plan on social media. Because for me, the stick of not honouring my word of what I stated publicly was a big motivator for making it happen.

Another external accountability action I put into place was locking in regular time with a book writing mentor. I had to show up to do the work, and the job got done.

Some of the ways to build in accountability are:

- Make your goal public
- Get a coach or join a mastermind accountability group
- Engage the support of a friend as an accountability buddy
- Understand your stick (meaning what is the driving pain that makes you want to complete this goal)
- Understand your carrot (what will it mean for you when this goal has been achieved)
- Adopt a not-negotiable mindset of no matter what, this will be done

Celebrating your way to success

The best part about undertaking and achieving a goal is who you become in the process. For many, it is easy to forget to celebrate the many little wins along the way; in other words – to enjoy the journey.

For me, celebrating the little wins along the way was the process of reviewing the successes, a-ha moments and challenges after each writing session. This allowed me to acknowledge and track all the expected and unexpected ways that I improved my focus and grew, not only as a writer but as a communicator, entrepreneur and human being.

Setting a big goal and working through it to achieve it will always be the best personal journey that you can embark upon.

THE HAZARDS AHEAD

Even with the perfect plan and framework to set and achieve any goal of your heart's desire – if it was this simple, then why are we not all achieving our goals?

Why are so many quitting halfway through, if not before even starting?

You will be your biggest challenge to overcome

It is not our circumstances, it is not our environment, and it is not for lack of resources. What it comes down to are the thoughts and beliefs we hold between our ears.

The first question we have to ask is this: where does our commitment lie? Is it to our dreams and desired goals?

Or is it our commitment to the current narrative, self-talk and limiting beliefs that hold us back?

Is it the reluctance of letting go of what is, for fear of not knowing who we would be without this current story?

This will trip us up before we even start.

Stepping Beyond Your Comfort Zone

> *"The cave you fear to enter holds the treasure you seek."*
> *~ Joseph Campbell*

The growth journey is a physical and emotional movement from comfort to discomfort, from known to unknown. It is about letting go of thoughts, habits and routines ingrained as a daily part of our lives, and at times, to the point of defining our identity.

It is an ending of sorts, therefore, a reluctance to let it go.

This appears differently for different people.

For those who are absolutely reluctant to let go, it shows up as a paralysis of action. In other words, they speak of their goals but fail to take any action or steps towards them.

It is Possible

For some, the struggle starts the moment they falter when something complex or challenging is presented. This is the mindset of someone who wants things to be easy while avoiding discomfort.

Another way it can show up is to avoid looking bad, fear of failure or a less than perfect first attempt. This can happen despite knowing that first attempts are rarely perfect and need practice to improve.

Another type of mindset is where one is triggered as the results of their work start to present themselves. This is where self-sabotaging behaviours kick in. It is due to being uneasy with success, receiving or feeling unworthy.

This commonly presents itself as imposter syndrome.

No matter how a person may block their progress, it predominantly comes down to their thoughts and beliefs. The narrative will identify whether a mindset is committed to the problem (stuck) or to the solution (growth).

Reaching the edge of our comfort zone will trigger us.

Author and relationship coach Gay Hendrichs refers to this as "Upper Limiting". Researcher and author Dr Joe Dispenza calls it "banging into yourself". Author and speaker Bob Proctor refers to it as "reaching the edge of your terror barrier".

No matter what you call it, it comes down to the feeling of fear and anxiety just before making a significant breakthrough.

> *"We must all suffer from one of two pains: the pain of discipline or the pain of regret. The difference is discipline weighs ounces while regret weighs tons."*
>
> *~ Jim Rohn*

Imposter Syndrome

The best way to overcome any form of self-sabotage is to work through the discomfort.

The only way through is through.

The term Imposter Syndrome was first used in 1978 in an academic article by Dr. Pauline Rose Clance and Suzanne A Imes, after interviewing 150 high achieving women.

For the most part, the women observed had everything working in their favour. They had come from well-educated and successful families who grew up in nice neighbourhoods. They were healthy, financially secure, had access to every opportunity and had a proven track record of success and academic achievement.

She noticed that they didn't believe in their ability and would say things like, "I'm going to fail this class", when all of the evidence she observed did not indicate that this was the case.

The Imposter Syndrome refers to high achieving individuals marked by an inability to internalise their accomplishments and persistent fear of being exposed as a fraud.

Clance has since said that calling it a syndrome was incorrect. Today, she actually refers to it as the Imposter Phenomenon because it is so common.

In her initial research, she concluded that it was more common for women since success for women is contradicted by societal expectations, as well as their own internalised self-evaluation.

More recently, however, it has been found that nearly everyone is affected by it in dozens of demographic groups, including men.

Some ways that Imposter Syndrome shows itself are:

- Comparing yourself to others, but you are not equal to them. Often experienced by high achievers in their fields or peer groups
- Feeling like your success is due to luck
- Feeling foolish or uncomfortable describing your achievements
- Not deserving or worthy or smart enough, haven't earned your stripes
- I'll get found out
- If people praise or congratulate me, I feel like I'm getting away with something
- Don't feel like success will come or last
- Don't feel like previous successes prove anything

In her book, The Secret Thoughts of Successful Women: why capable people suffer from the Imposter Syndrome and how to thrive in spite of it, author Valerie Young identified five types of the imposter.

Perfectionist *"I should have done better, mistakes are unacceptable"* – never being good enough.

Expert *"if I were naturally smart, I would know everything that there is to know"* – feeling completely unqualified.

Natural Genius *"if I were really smart, this would be effortless"* – if they have to work hard, they are no good.

Superhero *"if I were really competent, I'd be able to do it all"* – they feel undeserving.

Rugged Individualist *"the only achievement that really matters is the one I got myself"* – any task that has had a helping hand is not considered an achievement.

Journalling Exercise to overcome Imposter Syndrome

Pause and reflect on why you are feeling like an imposter. Which one of the five types of imposter do you identify with?

Is this really true?

If the answer is yes, what else could you think, do or tell yourself to reframe it differently?

If the answer is no, then what is a more empowering statement or thought?

Make a list of all the activities and actions you can take (including affirmations and mantras) to support and stack the evidence of your success.

Take action.

Progress is the Name of the Game

Understand that the journey is not a straight line. Between the start (exciting!) and the end (a celebration!), there is the messy middle. It is going to be awkward, clumsy, and your first efforts will more than likely suck.

The journey of learning something new has a ratio of more failed attempts than successes in the beginning. With intentional and daily practice, the balance starts to adjust to fewer failures and more successful attempts.

If you are not struggling or failing at the beginning of your journey, then chances are you are not stretching far beyond your comfort zone.

Intentional and consistent practice is where skills are developed. And remember, there is no such thing as failure. There is only feedback.

In a nutshell, it is through the messy middle where the magic and growth happens.

Planting Seeds for Success

Setting Yourself Up for Success

"The way we spend our time defines who we are."
~ Jonathan Estrin

Setting yourself up for success is having foundational practices, rituals, routines, set thoughts and behavioural guidelines, all designed to guide you towards your goals.

A solid daily routine and practice eliminate decision fatigue, mental clutter, and second-guessing as your next step. These are all the things that derail the best of intentions.

The best thing about having these foundational practices is that the outcome is already declared as achieved. The framework is a reminder and guideline of who we show up as. Think of it as your road map or GPS, telling you what to do and guiding you towards your destination.

A lack of complete or consistent success practices is one of the biggest reasons people do not achieve their goals. Often attributed to failure is this commonly accepted excuse: I don't have enough time.

Practice for Success

> "Don't judge each day by the harvest you reap but
> by the seeds that you plant."
> ~ Robert Louis Stevenson

A successful practice is any activity which when undertaken, contributes towards your health in mind, body and spirit, and when practised consistently, moves you towards your goals.

Individual activities are part of the sum of the whole. In general, a practice has an overarching theme and focus, but is a part of the bigger picture. It benefits as a stand-alone activity but comes into its own when performed consistently and in concert with the other practices.

For example, going for a walk has benefits for physical health and getting your energy moving. Meditation benefits the mind to experience calm and inner stillness.

Each practice on its own will move and contribute you towards a bigger goal; however, you fast-track the results when combining multiple practices.

Success practices include:

- Tracking, measuring and reviewing data
- Meditation, focused breathing, visualisation
- Journalling – gratitude, forgiveness
- Planning – goal setting, vision boarding
- Exercise – walking, stretching, Qigong
- Nourishment - drinking water, eating healthy food
- Prayers, mantras, affirmations
- Rest and recovery
- Play – fun and fulfilment
- Education and development – reading, training, podcasts
- Giving and contribution - time, knowledge, money

Planning and Scheduling for Success

It is said that if you fail to plan, you plan to fail. This is because our time and energy on a day-to-day basis are consumed by what is in front of us. When we fail to plan and schedule our lives to move us towards our goals, we become victims of living a life based on external circumstances.

The benefit of an overall plan, broken down into milestones and scheduled into our calendar, is a step-by-step, paint-by-numbers roadmap for success. All you have to do is show up and do what is scheduled for that day.

Key areas of planning are:

- Meal plans
- Reading and education
- Daily and weekly schedule
- Business and career plan
- Financial plan
- Exercise plan
- Social and holiday calendar
- Health and medical plan

Tracking for Success

There is a common flawed belief that there is not enough time, that we need more of it, and that it is working against us.

Yet the question is when we all have the same 24 hours in our day, why is it that Person A has a different level of productivity to Person B?

It has got nothing to do with the number of tasks or level of responsibility. What it comes down to is their relationship with time. The belief of a solid or a poor relationship with time comes down to fact-driven knowledge of how one utilises their time in relation to their results.

Most of my students and clients have never considered or thought about how they manage themself in relation to time. In the worst-case scenario they are overwhelmed, stressed, and feel hopeless in their lack of productivity.

As an observer, I've noticed a common pattern in which most of their time is spent putting out fires and reacting to events. Their day runs them – they have very little control, and generally, life is chaos.

The good news is that the solution is simple, and the starting point of this is to understand how they are currently spending their time. And this is why we always start with a time-tracking exercise.

> *"What gets measured gets improved."*
> *~ Peter Drucker*

Daily tracking of activity and results – whether related to money, health or relationships – is the process of monitoring and recording your activities and results. It identifies what is working and what is not, allowing you to review, assess and adjust before it becomes a significant problem.

There is a reason why tracking (food, time and money diaries) is a core component of any successful transformation program.

Tracking the following habits will provide:

- Food - provides insights to what, when and why you eat.
- Sleep - provides data of quantity and quality of sleep.
- Money - reveals your money relationship.
- Emotions - reveals triggers and underlying thoughts.
- Exercise - provides the data of regularity, duration and effort.

When you put all of this information together (and our practice is to have two weeks of data to work with), you pick up patterns and behaviours and can see how one area of life or activity can affect another. For example, it may result in more emotional outbursts or emotional eating on days with a lack of sleep. The data before you will allow you to put together a pattern of triggered behaviours.

The reason we track this data rather than rely on our memory and assessment is because, depending on our emotional state, we can overestimate and beat ourselves up about how poor we are about things, we underestimate or can be in denial or fear. Basically, we are flawed in our memory and recall.

The Importance of Tracking and Measuring

> *"Drop by drop is the water pot filled."*
> ~ Buddha

Tracking is not a once and done process; if you look at any successful individual, you will find that planned days and tracking are built into how they live.

Tracking is not just about improving. It is also an early warning system to help you course-correct before things go too far off track.

For example, had I been tracking my weight, nutrition intake, the quantity of alcohol consumption, and lack of exercise. I would not have found myself sitting in the doctor's office, horrified by the number on the scales, the poor state of my health and the gloomy direction of my future.

This situation wasn't just with my health. It was also reflected in the state of my finances and relationships.

Not tracking the results of daily events in my life was the metaphorical ostrich with its head in the sand.

Tracking removes the overthinking and eliminates the excuses. It either happened, or it hasn't. You either did or you didn't.

Being clear about your daily goals and keeping a record of the activity towards them:

- Motivates you
- Keeps you accountable
- Helps you see your progress
- Allows you to course-correct before you go too far off track

The fastest way to create change in your life is to:

- Get clear on what you want (set goals)
- Make a plan to achieve them
- Take daily action as required towards your goals
- Be accountable – TRACK YOUR PROGRESS
- Based on your progress, course-correct

The Two-Week Tracking Exercise

The task is to track two weeks of sleep, food and activity. It is not negotiable to have two weeks of tracked data before moving onto the next stage.

There is a very deliberate reason for this. Tracking everything you do every day for two weeks can be highly challenging and confronting to do, and while you may start off with enthusiasm and motivation, it soon reveals when this wanes with lack of commitment and follow-through (for some, it is day one).

By using different colours to track the different activities, you will gain a solid visual of what you are doing with your time.

Two Weeks of Consistent Data

There is a purpose behind this method. How a student undertakes this task can be revealing in itself. For example, suppose I have a student who consistently fails to complete their tracking data daily as instructed. As a coach, it highlights the level of commitment to the solution versus their comfort level living with the pain. The inconvenience of tracking and recording is far more uncomfortable than their current pain and chaos.

> *"You'll never change your life until you change something you do daily. The secret of your success is found in your daily routine."*
>
> ~ *John C. Maxwell*

Fiona Redding

Weekly Schedule

Week beginning: ....   *Name:* ....

hours	Monday	Tuesday	Wednesday	Thursday	Friday	Saturday	Sunday
5 a.m							
6 a.m							
7 a.m							
8 a.m							
9 a.m							
10 a.m							
11 a.m							
12 a.m							
1 p.m							
2 p.m							
3 p.m							
4 p.m							
5 p.m							
6 p.m							
7 p.m							
8 p.m							
9 p.m							
10 p.m							
11 p.m							
12 p.m							
1 a.m							
2 a.m							
3 a.m							
4 a.m							

What to Track

Sleep

Record wake up and sleep times, and we record this by shading in the corresponding time cells. This provides instant visual feedback. What we are looking for in sleep tracking is the inconsistency in bed-time and waking time. If there is inconsistency, this is the first task for correction.

There is a reason why sleep deprivation is a form of torture. It is the quickest way to break a person down mentally and physically. If you think back to any interrogation scene you have watched on television, the sleep deprived person is less likely to stick to their story, especially if it is a false narrative. The sleep deprived person is easily confused and open to misleading information.

Most bad decisions are made when we are fatigued.

Immunity is compromised when tired. Your body is under stress. With stress being the number one threat to heart health.

Sleep is a healing and recovery process and it is why there is so much discussion around sleep hygiene and the quality of sleep that we experience. It is during sleep that our body can heal and recover, and we can process the events of the day through our dreams.

Nutrition and Food

On the tracking sheet record what time you ate, whether it be a snack or a meal. On a separate sheet of paper, record what you ate, and why you are eating. Is it hunger, boredom, stress?

At this early stage of tracking data, what we are looking for here is the time and patterns of when we eat. Like sleep, what we feed our body, how often and how much has a direct impact on how we feel and respond to events. On a greater scale, it will reveal whether you eat mindfully or mindlessly.

Tasks and How We Spend Our Day

Make a note and block in the different tasks and activities done throughout the day.

- Work
- Admin
- Exercise
- Cooking
- Family
- Travel
- Reading, rest, alone time

Keep it simple. The objective here is to get a snapshot of real time data of how we spend our day. The simple legend means we can block activities, making it easier to track.

Just do this for two weeks and you will notice an improvement (this is the observer effect in play). Having an awareness of what you are doing will improve your behaviour and decision-making.

Things to look out for:

- Not tracking in real time. Thinking you can batch it in arrears or you can insert the data before you have taken action.

  This is avoidance and taking a shortcut, as opposed to being fully committed and active in the process.

- Fudging the figures, because of self-judgement and denial. The goal here is to bring everything to the table so that you can clearly see the real picture of what is happening.

- Wanting the end result, without being willing to take the first step.

Assessing the Data

The first thing to look for is a consistent and healthy sleep cycle, and if it is not, that is the focus and task for the next two weeks.

The next one is consistency and quality of nutrition. The two best places to start from here are consistent meal times and being organised, e.g. if you are deciding to eat on the run or meal planning. Nutrition can also include hydration and your water intake.

With the data that has been gathered with regards to the tasks you undertake, categorise the activity and then apply a value to it.

Family time is high priority, high return

Business sales is high priority, high return

The objective here is to look at the data, and ask: "How can I improve upon this; how can I be smarter with my time?"

For example:

Sleep: if your sleep cycle is inconsistent, your next best move is to set and do a consistent sleep routine, with the appropriate hours needed.

If your sleep routine is good, the next move is to check the quality of your sleep.

If the quality of sleep is where you want it, the next step is to look at your bed-time mindfulness practice (preparation for bed).

Meal times: If the times of when you eat are all over the place, your next best practice and task is to aim for consistent meal times.

If your meal times are consistent, are you making on the spot decisions about what to eat or do you have a pre-set meal plan? If not, your next best move is meal planning.

If you eat a meal plan, your next best step would be to look at how you can improve the quality and nutrition value of your food.

Activity: If your activity is reactive, and you generally wake up without a plan for the day, your next best move is to group and schedule activities into set time blocks.

If you already schedule your activities but have trouble sticking to them, your next best move is to practice your non-negotiable schedule.

If you find your schedule is disrupted with non-negotiable activities (e.g. working at home with children), then your next best move is to create a schedule with more flexibility and space.

What Does Tracking Do?

Tracking for me started off as simply as using a set of scales to measure my weight. It kept me accountable and motivated. When the numbers were heading in the wrong direction, it was immediate feedback for me to review and adjust my daily choices.

When the numbers reflected a positive result, it built confidence, kept me energised and motivated me to keep going.

Let's have a conversation about the scales. This is one of the biggest anxieties for people who feel less than comfortable about their weight, and is usually an indicator of avoiding the hard conversations with self.

What is misplaced here is that we allow the numbers presented to determine whether we are going to have a positive or a negative thought, which then determines whether we are going to have a good or a bad day.

In other words, the scales control and determine the type of mood and day you are going to have.

This happens because there is no plan with how to deal with the information presented, including building up the confidence to step on the scales. Most people will have anxious thoughts leading up to the scales, however what you want to do instead is to centre yourself and know that this is simply a data collection exercise.

An interesting observation is that how you feel and respond to the numbers on a scale is also revealing of the underlying behaviour of placing the responsibility of how you feel onto external factors.

The scale is a data providing resource. Are you going to get upset when your kitchen scales show that your food item weighs differently than what you want, or your fuel tank indicator points to empty?

The diet and food industry has fed into the fear and insecurities of the scales, often giving the advice to ignore scales and numbers – as opposed to learning how to work with the data.

For example, one is that you don't need the numbers on the scales, just go with how you feel. We can trick ourselves into "feeling good" or "I've earned it" to justify actions that do not serve us in a healthy way.

Or this one. The scales trigger me and make me feel bad about myself. The problem with this is that you are presented with an opportunity to expose a belief or a feeling and instead of embracing it and working through it, you are avoiding it and therefore reinforcing it.

Ultimately, if the scales trigger you, or you have a thought or trepidation or fear about jumping on the scales, or what the numbers will reveal. You want to embrace this as an opportunity to learn how to love and accept yourself even more.

Overcome the Fear of the Scales

- Set up the routine as to when and how often you will weigh yourself. I recommend to my students to do this weekly – first thing on a Wednesday morning – naked and after you've been to the bathroom.

  The reason we do this is first of all to create a set routine of a weigh-in day, and by doing it at the same time and as a familiar bathroom practice, the numbers will be more consistent.

- Before you step on the scales, check-in with the self-talk and align yourself with a neutrally emotional position.

  You are here to collect data and what is presented before you will either confirm to keep up the good work, or adjust what you have been doing.

  "This is me just collecting data." If the numbers don't go your way, check-in with what you are feeling and remind yourself that: "This is okay and I have the data to figure this out. I will figure this out."

- Record the weight and journal your thoughts and feelings about it. If you are feeling really good about the result, you want to check-in, journal and acknowledge all the things that you did that worked to get this result.

  If the numbers were not what you were hoping for, then journal through the triggers and feelings around that and have an honest conversation with yourself. Did I stick to the plan last week? And if not, what will I do differently this week?

The number on the scale is simply one set of data which provides feedback as to whether you are on track, or need to course-correct your action.

There may be fluctuation, and that is why the data from the scales is often referenced against other data measures, for example: measurements, body fat ratio, flexibility, strength and blood tests.

The goal here is to get really comfortable with stepping onto the scales. For some to get to this point, the practice of weighing-in every day to trigger and work through the emotion was the best way to do it.

Interestingly, when you have consistent data, you begin to see the patterns and fluctuations of the body according to its cycle.

Without the right attitude, self-talk and game plan – even for a person who sees a weight loss – it can trigger a self-sabotage of over-eating to celebrate.

Prior to my doing the inner work around my relationship with the scales, I believed and brought into the notion that the thing was evil and to be avoided at all cost.

My Morning Success Routine

> *"The way you start your day determines how well you live your day."*
> ~ Robin Shama

While throwing myself wholly and solely into my practices, I was still on the hunt for other clues to success. I discovered the common thread amongst happy and successful people, and anyone who had turned their life around, was a set morning routine.

What I mean by a morning routine is a set of rituals and practices, each designed to clear the mind and strengthen the body, while reminding and aligning our thoughts with the bigger vision.

Think of it like a morning practice that recalibrates you emotionally, mentally, physically and spiritually in the direction of your goals.

Ultimately what this does is sets the foundations of your day up for success.

The power of undertaking this daily morning routine is in the forming of the habit. The elevated way of thinking, being and doing ingrains your identity. This really is the easiest and best way to bring forth our best selves.

It has been proven beyond a shadow of a doubt that we will create the life that matches who we think we are. Life before my morning rituals was chaos, to say the least. Rather than me running the day, the day was running me.

My day would start when my children woke up (they were my alarm clock). Pretty much from the get-go, I was in reaction mode. What I did was dictated by what I had to do based on external factors. I found myself with various levels of resentment because there just never seemed to be any space for me. On most days, it felt like there were no moments of peace.

This approach of just going at it and being utterly reactive without any mental downtime, let alone space to even think about future goals and plans, created a high-stress environment, resulting in me showing up with an underlying and brewing attitude of anger and resentment.

A pivotal turning point came one morning when my three-year-old son was doing what three-year-olds do and not putting on his shoes on my timeline. Before I knew it, I was in the midst of an uncontrolled and emotional outburst, directed at this beautiful little boy.

I recall feeling the veins in my neck straining and popping out; I could feel the heat in my face. And even though I could see his little face, and he was looking at me with a look of complete terror, I couldn't stop. I was not in control.

The thing was not the thing. It had nothing to do with the shoes. The steady build-up of stress and feelings of resentment and anger had created this explosion of emotion towards my son. I knew there was a problem, and something had to change. Fast.

I realised my morning routine was one of reactive mode. I would wake up and go straight into the day in reaction and with an underlying sense of resentment of waking up at 6am – not because I wanted to, but because it's when my children woke up.

I had started a simple meditation practice in the evening to help me get to sleep. It was working quite well, and it was pretty evident that morning routines were a powerful success practice. It made perfect sense to incorporate a morning routine into my life.

The problem was, I had a resistance to having to get up any earlier than I already was (which, by the way, is still one of the most common objections I hear when introducing the concept of a morning routine).

It isn't surprising to say that my first attempt at incorporating a morning success routine was an unmitigated disaster, possibly adding more stress than was already being experienced. Rather than looking at my morning structure to start with, I just added more tasks to what was already a chaotic routine.

There I was trying to be all zen, meditating, having peaceful thoughts... with my children clamouring for my attention and me getting angry that they were not giving me space. It is worth noting that they were two and three years old at the time.

I realised that if I was going to have any chance of succeeding, I needed to do things differently. The interesting thing is that when my intention and mission was focused on succeeding and what I needed to do to set myself up for success, the resistance was no longer there.

Looking back, I realise that this old way of thinking was simply me trying to control a situation that I did not like – another lesson in how letting go of the need to control created more ease in my life.

While my morning success routine has evolved over the years, this was what my first morning success routine looked like:

- 5am wake up and out of bed an hour before my children
- Drink a glass of hot lemon water
- 10-minute meditation, eventually expanding to 30+ minutes
- Shower and get dressed
- Go for a walk with the children, as early as possible

As simple as this routine seems, what it gave me was space, peace and a sense of responsiveness and control. I felt more empowered and ready for whatever the day presented.

My interaction with my children was a lot more loving and peaceful first thing in the morning. We were all a lot happier. My children are my highest priority and greatest love. I was now greeting and meeting them each morning with love and big hugs, rather than my frustrations and anger at where I was in life.

This was an instant shift.

Over the years, my morning routine has evolved, with the addition of the following:

- 15 minutes of focused breathing practice
- Daily success affirmations and prayers
- Writing out my Major Definite Purpose
- Writing out my daily goals
- Journalling
- Gratitude
- Minimum 30-minute walk (I aim for 10,000 steps a day)
- 15 minutes gentle exercise (stretches or chigung)
- Green smoothie

While it seems like a lot, I have fine-tuned this practice down to between 90 minutes and no more than two hours. While two hours can seem like a big chunk of time out of my day, it really is the foundation of getting more done, staying focused, productive and efficient.

I feel in control of my days. I feel mentally grounded to take on whatever the day will bring, physically energised and connected to my mission. When I'm consistent with my morning practice, I show up as the best version of myself, and it sets me up to continue at this level throughout the day.

As important as the morning routine is, it is worth noting that I do bookend with a shorter meditation and a reflection practice at the end of the day. Bookending the day allows me to review and close the day (closing off any open loops) and preparing myself for a restful sleep.

Morning Success Routine – It's Not a One Size Fits All

Over the years, I have had to adapt and adjust what I was doing to make it work for my family and me. Having a morning routine is not negotiable. However, it is also essential to have the flexibility of what it looks like, based on my schedule and other life requirements.

Morning routines look different for different people. What works for me (i.e. meditation, 5am rise and gratitude journalling) may not be the practice that works for another.

For example, I have a friend whose morning routine is to wake up and get the body moving in exercise as her first morning success practice. Where I like to sit in a quiet space for meditation, her meditation is incorporated into her activity (making it an active meditation).

These are both still focused practices. They just look slightly different but have been incorporated into the way that works best for each person. The takeaway of creating your successful morning practice is to know that this is a block of time dedicated for you, and multi-tasking defeats its purpose.

Look to this day

For it is life, the very life of life.

In its brief course

Lie all the verities and realities of your existence.

The bliss of growth,

The glory of action,

The splendour of achievement

Are but experiences of time.

For yesterday is but a dream

And tomorrow is only a vision;

And today well-lived makes

Yesterday a dream of happiness

And every tomorrow a vision of hope.

Look well therefore to this day;

Such is the salutation to the ever-new dawn!

~ Kalidasa

How to Create Your Morning Success Routine

*"The breeze at dawn has secrets to tell you.
Don't go back to sleep."*
~ Rumi

Design your morning success routine. Remember, you don't have to do it all at once. My recommendation and what I start my students with is the critical four: meditation, gratitude practice, set daily goals and daily walks.

- Assess your environment and if (like me) you have to get up before anyone else to have that space, decide what time you need to get up.

- It may also help to have a conversation with your housemates (big and little) to explain what you are doing and why it is essential to you.

- Your morning routine starts the night before. Once you know what time you need to get up, work out how much sleep you need to determine your bed-time.

- Commit to this. It may take a little practice, but I promise you it is worth it. Make getting enough sleep your priority.

Aside from starting your day on the right foot, there have been countless studies and evidence of the health benefits of having enough sleep. If you are a night owl or constantly operating on minimum sleep, I highly recommend you get acquainted with the conversation and the benefits surrounding sleep hygiene. A quick Google search will give you plenty of resources to work with.

Just do it. Take the pressure off yourself. What you do may be imperfectly perfect. Doing it is better than thinking and talking about it.

Mindset and Heartset

*"The truth **will** set you free."*
~ John 8:32

To really understand what mindset and heartset are and their roles in our wellbeing and health, we need to step into metaphysical language, concepts, and teachings.

The contents of this chapter may take some of you outside of your normal realm of thought and into conversations often referred to as "woo-woo". Be open.

Metaphysics is a branch of philosophy. It is about going beyond the limitations of our current thinking and outside our current perception of reality, to open ourselves to a higher level of consciousness and awareness.

What has been provided here is an introduction, and my understanding of some key fields and teachings of metaphysics.

> "My definition of metaphysics would be the search for absolute reality. The search for: Who am I? Where have I been? Where am I going? What is the relationship of man, mind and the Universe?
>
> If you can answer these questions, you can find your place in life. If you can't, then it doesn't matter, you're just a wanderer."
>
> ~Dr Paul Leon Masters

The Universal Laws

> *"If you wish to understand the Universe, think of energy, frequency and vibration."*
>
> ~ Nikola Tesla

Life is orchestrated through a set of natural laws that govern the Universe and life on Earth. The Universal Laws are unchanging, immutable and always working with us, whether we are aware of them or not. Harnessed correctly, they work to master your life.

Like most people, my introduction was through the Law of Attraction. It opened my mind to a realm of possibility beyond what I knew and what I thought I knew. What really clinched the deal was that I learned that I had the power to intentionally call in what I desired, even as I had been inadvertently using it to attract what I didn't want.

In a nutshell, to step into a mindset of possibility, I simply needed to step out of myself and my conditioned view of the world. By doing this, I would be connecting to something bigger than myself.

How do people refer to and use them?

The Universal Laws are ancient and eternal, and we can find reference to them – and their cause – philosophically, culturally and spiritually throughout human history via:

- The Bible
- Stoic philosophy
- Bhagavad Gita
- Yoga
- Hawaiian culture and practice of Ho'oponopono
- Hermetic philosophy
- Rosicrucians
- Modern-day success principles are guided by the Universal Laws

How many are there?

There are millions of Universal Laws. Everything in the Universe is part of nature, and the laws govern it all.

The introduction of Universal Laws into the mainstream was made popular through the Rhonda Byrnes book, and subsequent documentary: "The Secret". For many, this is the only law they knew, and they were unaware that there were many more.

Teaching and coaching through the Laws became popular through self-development and life coaches, each picking their magical number of laws to focus on (the most common being 7, 12 or 14).

While this list is not complete, the Laws mentioned here are the ones I learned of, and embraced for my journey.

The laws are straightforward, and it is within their simplicity that their power lies.

The Law of Connection

This Law states that all things, all thoughts, all actions, all events are inter-connected. There is a connection between anything and everything else – including with all of the Universal Laws. All is one.

How to work with it

Recognise that we are all connected. See yourself in others, and see others in yourself. The past, present and future are connected. Recognise the connection between your thoughts, emotions and your results.

The Law of Love

The Universal Law of Love, first and foremost, is the love of God, the Creator, source and Universe. It is the essence of all relationships, including the one with self.

How to work with it

Operate, walk and work from a place of love for self and others. Be compassionate. Always be kind. Choose love.

The Law of Attraction

Like attracts like. We are creators of our life and world, and how we do this is by attracting what matches our vibration. To understand your current frequency, look at the results of what you are currently attracting.

How to work with it

Recognise where you are attracting what you want and where you are not. Get clear and start focusing on what you want. Believe you can have it. Implement practices to raise your vibration so that you match the frequency to attract what you want.

The Law of Reciprocity

The Law of Reciprocity is about being useful and of value. When we give something freely, we can know it will come back in another form or source.

How to work with it

In relationships and business, operate, deliver and be of value without expectation (when you expect something in return, you are operating outside of this Law – it becomes a transaction).

The Law of Gratitude

The Law of Gratitude is to be appreciative and thankful because when you count your blessings, the more you see what you have to bless. At the same time, it increases your vibration to attract more of what you desire.

How to work with it

Implement a daily gratitude practice, including expressing gratitude in advance for that which you want to become and to attract. Say thank you for everything.

Gratitude can be as simple as repeating thank you, thank you and thank you – while meaning it.

The Law of Action

The Law of Action states that you must act and take the necessary steps to achieve your desired outcome. Remember that the journey of a thousand miles always begins with a single step.

How to work with it

Once the goal has been set, create an action plan with milestones to achieve it (this is your road map). Do the first step.

The Law Cause and Effect (Karma)

Like a pendulum, this Law states that every action has a reaction or a consequence. We reap what we sow. There is no escape from the results of our thoughts and actions.

How to work with it

Recognise that everything that happens for you is a result of your past thinking, actions and behaviour. Change your thoughts, actions and behaviour to change the experience you are having. Employ The Big Guns.

The Law of Forgiveness

The Law of Forgiveness is about letting go of, making right or correcting mistakes, wrong-doings and errors, recognising that we all make mistakes, and it is through our mistakes that we have the opportunity to learn and grow.

How to work with it

Let go of the need to hold on to past mistakes, hurts, shame and memories, free yourself, live in peace and raise your vibration.

The Law of Perpetual Transmutation of Energy

This Law states that everything in the Universe is energy, and energy is constantly moving, evolving and fluctuating. Energy cannot be created or destroyed, it always is, and always will be.

In a nutshell, everything is energy and energy changes form.

How to work with it

Nothing is permanent. Things are always changing. Use your current experience as the contrast to fuel a different reality. Change your thoughts, feelings and actions to make it happen. Appreciate and be grateful for where you are now

The Law of Germination

The Law of Germination holds that there is a period of time required for something to become or to manifest.

How to work with it

Be patient. Move from a need for instant gratification to a solid commitment to the process. The ground needs to be prepared before planting a seed. A seed planted requires water, sunlight and the right nutrients to grow into a tree that bears fruit.

A baby takes nine months from germination to birth, and then 18 plus years to reach maturity.

The Law of Correspondence

The Law of Correspondence is the communication between our inner and outer world, and our higher and lower self. It states that the world is our mirror. The outer world is a reflection of the inner world. As within, so without. As above, so below.

How to work with it

Your external world is feedback as to how you are showing up.

If you don't like what you are seeing or experiencing, focus on improving your inner world first. Be honest with yourself about what you are really thinking and feeling, what your inner world is telling you, and create the change from within. From here, you will see and experience the corresponding shift in the external world.

The Law of Compensation

This Law states that you will always be compensated for your efforts and contribution. As Ralph Waldo Emerson once quoted,: "The whole of what we know is a system of compensation. Every suffering is rewarded; every sacrifice made up; every debt paid."

How to work with it

Be a contributor and put in an effort with a good attitude.

The Law of Polarity

This Law states that everything has two poles – all things have an opposite. There is duality in everything; what appears to be the opposite are two inseparable parts of the same thing.

One does not exist without the other. In Chinese culture, it is referred to as yin and yang. The white is in the black, and the black is in the white.

How to work with it

Know that without sadness, we cannot experience happiness. Without night, there is no day. To step into our highest self, we need to recognise that there is a lower self.

If you don't like what you are experiencing, look for the opposite in it, and choose to focus there. The cup is both half full, and half empty. Both are true. Pick the better focus.

The Law of Giving and Receiving

This Law is about the Universal economic flow of energy and the balance of exchange. Everything in the Universe operates through this dynamic exchange. Giving and receiving are different aspects of the flow of energy in the Universe, yet a balance needs to be met for it to work in harmony.

How to work with it

Be conscious of the balance of your giving and receiving. Give freely and without thought for return, and equally, allow yourself to receive.

The Law of Gender

This is the Law of Creation. In all creation, there is a male and female. In each creation, there is masculine and feminine energy.

Masculine energy is action-orientated. It has doing, protective, planning and giving characteristics. Feminine energy is receptive. It is a "being and presence" energy.

Both are powerful in their own right. It is the combination of both, in the correct dose for the situation at hand, that can harness the true power of this Law.

How to work with it

Recognise and know your masculine and feminine traits. Learn and study their characteristics and where they best serve or damage a situation or relationship.

The Law of Vibration

As the Universe is made of energy, and energy is constantly moving, the Law of Vibration says that everything moves at a specific frequency. The frequency we are operating at determines our experience.

How to work with it

Become a vibrational match for that which you desire. And you do this by thinking, feeling and acting as the person who has already achieved that goal.

Same, same... but different

Like the interconnectedness of the Universe, the Laws are connected.

For example, the Law of Polarity and the Law of Gender can appear to be interchangeable yet have specific differences for their purpose.

The Law of Polarity is about opposites and the need for each to exist to create the whole (two sides of the same coin), whereas the Law of Gender is about the two different energy types and how they work together.

Working with and Against the Laws

Understand the Universal Laws, and not only will you change the way you live, but you will also see the perfect harmony of nature and your role within it.

Working against them still creates a result – it will simply be the one you don't want.

You cannot get around them, and there is a price to pay for violating them – you are going against the Laws of nature.

Working with the Laws is a matter of understanding the concept and using it to guide your everyday decisions and actions.

Energy/Vibration/Frequency

The idea of energy, vibration and frequency are now part of our common language, and the words are used interchangeably, especially in discussions of manifestation and emotional health. I believe that there is value in understanding the subtle differences and how they work together.

Energy

Energy refers to the concept of force that has the potential for causing change, and hence why it is said that energy is the cause of any change.

Vibration

Vibration refers to the vibrating movement of atoms and particles caused by energy. Energy is movement, and the process of movement is the process of creation.

Frequency

Frequency is the measurement rate of vibration. In a nutshell: energy is the cause, vibration is the reaction, and frequency is the measurement.

ENERGY - What is it?

Energy is movement, and the process of movement is the process of creation. There are many different forms of energy:

- Thermal
- Radiant
- Chemical
- Nuclear
- Electrical
- Motion
- Sound
- Elastic
- Gravitational

In the realm of possibility and personal transformation, when we speak of energy, we refer to the mental, emotional and physical bodies, which then creates a metaphysical effect in our life.

Energy can be generated, harnessed and redirected.

Optimal Energetic Health

Energetic health can be measured by assessing our emotional, mental, physical and spiritual health. This can often be referred to in general terms as the mind-body-spirit connection.

Stagnant or stuck energy in one of these areas will affect the others, eventually disrupting health in all areas.

Everything is linked. Therefore this is true when it comes to practices of optimal energetic health-focused in one area, flowing onto the other three regions.

Signs of depleted or stagnant energetic flow:

- Mental chaos and clutter
- Lethargic thinking and/or being
- Emotionally stuck or reactive
- Feelings of disconnection
- Tense and wired in body and thought, feelings of panic
- Anxious and overwhelmed
- Myriad physical pain and ailments
- Surrounded by drama

On the other end of energetic health, we are now looking at the best version of ourselves – what I believe should be our ultimate goal, mission and purpose (because this is where everything is possible).

Signs of optimal energetic flow:

- A feeling of being fully charged (in mind, body and spirit)
- Clarity of thought, with firm direction and decisiveness
- Physical health – clear skin, a vibrant glow and alertness
- Empowered and empowering relationships
- Fully present in the now
- In a complete state of flow – operating in "the zone"
- Magnetism – being your luckiest and the magic just happens
- Emotionally intelligent and connected to all that is around you and within, without being controlled by it

Enhancing our Energy Source

It is disheartening to see how neglected and overlooked our energetic health is, especially for something that significantly impacts every aspect of our body, life, and relationships. Yet, it is something so quickly and easily improved.

Even though this process is fundamentally simple, what is uncovered in the process (the very thing most people are trying to avoid) is what makes it "difficult to do".

This is where the myth of it being a complicated process emerges from. I constantly hear the excuse of not being ready to start this journey because the student fears the painful process of having to "face their demons".

This could not be further from the truth. In fact, it is counter-productive to continue revisiting the trauma. This process is not about putting the spotlight on how one failed or what went wrong, as this only increases the self-talk of blame, shame and guilt.

It is about looking at the self in the now, the effectiveness of the current behaviours and actions, and showing up in our best version. A big part of this process is by releasing the constraints and stories of the past.

The "difficult" part is letting go of the stories that have been part of our narrative for far too long and changing them to something new.

Everybody wants the rewards, yet they don't want to do the work. This is why the self-help and diet industry is booming based on selling quick fixes and shortcuts, which leads you to believe that you can avoid the "hard" work.

You may get some results from this, yet in most cases, the change is temporary.

It is Possible

We all have access to an infinite and powerful source of energy. The difference between those who receive it in its complete and entire form (optimal energy flow) and those depleted is how they restrict themselves to receiving it.

Energy is powerful, pure and healthy – we don't heal energy. What is healed is the state of being that stops us from receiving it in its full form. This is what the language of "blocked" energy refers to.

This effectively is about practising the Law of Receiving.

We ask for what we want. We receive gifts for us in every moment, yet how many of us resist and repel it by dismissing, deflecting and downplaying an opportunity to receive. For example, think how well you received the last compliment you were given.

Masculine and Feminine - Higher

Masculine	Feminine
Logical Thought	Intuitive Feeling
Mind	Senses
Decisive	Creativity
Risk - Taking	Nurturing
Achieving (Goal Oriented)	Experincing
Controlling	Being
Competitive	Collaborative
Intellectual	Expressive
Giving	Receiving
Respectful	Empathetic
Inspiring	Trusting

Masculine and Feminine - Lower

Masculine	Feminine
Controlling	Controlling
Dominant	Insecure
Hard	Passive - aggressive
Overbearing	Belittling
Aggressive	Bitchy
Emotionless	Timid
Heartless	Manipulative
Abusive	Naive
Competitive (when not called for)	Gullible
Forceful	Erratic
Rigid	Illogical

How to Clear Blocked Energy

There are numerous healing modalities and practices for removing energetic blocks, and what I have found to be the most effective pathway is to have a game plan. This is why the work of The Happiness Hunter is structured with daily actions and practices to cover all bases (we throw everything at it).

The best place to start is understanding where you currently are and where you want to go. Go back to the list of signs of depleted and optimal energetic flow, and put a tick alongside the ones that match your state now.

From here, set your intention of where you want to be energetically, and formulate an action plan to achieve this.

As an example, The Happiness Hunter program includes the following practices:

Mind – goal setting, journalling, gratitude, affirmations

Body – movement (walk), drink water, nutrition, sleep, healing (e.g. Ajna Tibetan Healing, massage, chiropractor, kinesiology, acupuncture)

Spirit – meditation, prayer, visualisation, acts of kindness

Masculine and Feminine energy

What is it?

Unrelated to our gender, each of us has an energy source that falls into the category feminine or masculine. Depending on and driven by our day-to-day schedules and responsibilities, most of us will dominate in one. Both the feminine and masculine energies have higher and lower-level traits.

Masculine energy is action-orientated. It is very focused. It has doing, protective, planning and giving characteristics. Feminine energy is receptive. It is big-picture. It is a "being and presence" energy.

Both are powerful in their own right (at a constructive and deconstructive level), and it is in the combination of both, in the right dose for the situation at hand that can harness the true power for growth.

Leaning back / Leaning in

Leaning back (the feminine energy) in power is knowing that all is perfect as is. It is to be without an agenda, without trying to make anything happen. There is no push.

It is the act of receiving. It is worth noting that there are many moments in which we are not open to receiving – whether it be new ideas, abundance or love.

Leaning back is confidence in what is, without having to do anything or control it. It is a surrender. It lets go of the need for anything beyond this moment and that whatever happens, it will be perfect.

It is a sense of peace, calm and flow. It creates harmony.

How to practice leaning back

Physically lean back and inhale and exhale the breath deeply and slowly. Relax your neck and shoulders. Breathe into your body.

Focus on the moment. Notice if you are thinking about someone or something else other than the task before you – are you distracted?

Detach from the need for controlling or having expectations.

Leaning in

Leaning in (the masculine energy) is the doing and action energy.

Why master it?

It is the energy of projecting authority, confidence and getting things done. This is precisely the energy you want to be working with if you are interviewing for a job, leading a team or wanting to influence.

How to practice leaning in

Focus on the objective and core desires. Be assertive and decisive. Stand firm, with a solid posture. Maintain direct eye contact, and create an air and energy of confidence.

Take care and nurture those around you – step into the leadership and protective role. Masculine energy will attract feminine energy and vice versa.

Showing up intentionally versus mindlessly

There are scenarios in which it is evident as to which energy is required. For example, as a business owner or entrepreneur, your workday needs the doing, action-oriented energy of the masculine: the "hustle". However, go-go-go is not a sustainable strategy, as we know with the high levels of burn-out.

Allowing yourself to step into the feminine, trusting, allowing and receiving energy – taking action (masculine) and then letting go of the outcome (feminine) – is when you allow the process of creation to fully manifest.

A great example of this was shared with me by a coach of mine, Bernadette Doyle. Twenty something years ago, before mobile phones, she delivered sales training in Ireland in a large training room, using old school landlines.

One of the activities she had her students do was to make two phone calls and take two phone calls from other students on the course. What this meant was that if you were on the phone the whole time making calls (in the doing, action-oriented energy), your phone line would never be free to take the calls (in the passive, receiving energy).

Both are equally important.

As the one half of an intimate relationship, how you show up balances your partner's energy, i.e. feminine to masculine and masculine to feminine. This is where the energy works like a magnet drawing the opposites together.

Two of the same energies (masculine/masculine or feminine/feminine) will rarely work in harmony in intimate relationships.

Matching energies can work together and benefit other types of relationships, professional, business etc.

Balanced and Unbalanced

Without self-awareness, most of us operate from a dominant and default energetic base, often formed from past experiences, trauma or beliefs. Understanding whether this dominant trait is constructive or destructive for you comes down to your levels of peace, happiness and results with where you are at.

Balanced masculine/feminine energy is knowing which energy is required to work best concerning your surroundings and adjust according to the moment, person, or situation.

> *"When the only tool you have is a hammer,
> the whole world becomes a nail."*
> ~ unknown

An unbalanced operating energetic default is often defined by a lack of awareness or checking-in with yourself about how you are showing up. This is also the trait of someone operating from a place of survival mode, mistrust and fear.

How to Rebalance

Take a moment to pause, review the situation and get clear on what your desired outcome is. Remember, balanced energy is about knowing how to move in and out of masculine and feminine energy which can be a moment-to-moment action, depending on your particular scenario. There are no clear cut instructions for this; mastering it comes from self-awareness, awareness of desired outcome and practice.

The Passive - Assertive - Aggressive Spectrum

Passive	Assertive	Aggressive
Scared to speak up	Speaks openly	Interrupts and talks over others
Speaks softly or weakly	Speaks in a conversational tone	Speaks loudly
Hesitant speech, frequent pauses	Fluent speech, steady even pace	Fluent often abrupt, clipped, fast
Avoids eye contact	Makes and maintains good eye contact	Glares and stares
Reduces own self esteem	Increases own self-esteem	Reduces others self-esteem
Minimal facial expression	Facial expression matches the message	Intimidates through facial expression
Physically slouched and withdrawn	Relaxed with an open stance	Rigid, crossed-arms, invades space
Isolates from groups	Participates in groups	Controls groups
Values self less	Values self equally	Values self more
Put others needs first	Takes all need into account	Puts own needs first
Can't say no	Can say no in a calm and direct way	Says no aggressively or reactively
May not know or doesn't reach goals	Reaches goals without hurting others	Reaches goals but can hurt others
Aims to please others	Aims to express needs	Aims to win

Empowering Assertive Behaviour

When having conversations about masculine and feminine energy, it can also be helpful to look at the passive-assertive-aggressive behaviour spectrum.

When you consider behaviour through the lens of higher and lower masculine and feminine energy, you can see how the energetic position impacts your behaviour and how you are showing up.

Do some journaling on the following:

- Where does your behaviour sit (for the most part) on this spectrum?
- Where do you think others see you?
- Reflect on an example where you felt powerless (passive)
- Reflect on an example where you incorrectly used your power (aggressive)
- Reflect on an example where you behaved assertively
- What is your default energy source: masculine or feminine, higher or lower?
- What can you do to become more balanced and assertive in your behaviour?

An Introduction to the Aura

The aura is the energy field surrounding our physical body. All living things have an aura. They come in many colours and are considered to be an insight into our current state of wellbeing. While some people can see auras, most of us will feel them (think about the "vibe" you get from someone).

It is believed that there are seven layers of the aura (also known as bodies or planes). Each of these layers has a purpose, with the successive layers completely interpenetrating the layers underneath it, including the physical body.

Physical aura plane

Closest to the skin, this represents physical health.

Emotional aura plane

Corresponding with your emotions, this plane reflects your emotional state and changes colour depending on your mood.

Mental aura plane

The third layer outside of your body relates to logic, reasoning and thoughts.

Astral body aura plane

This plane represents your spiritual health and moves outward.

Etheric aura plane

Connected to psychic abilities, this plane connects you with other people's energy and those on a similar wavelength.

Celestial aura plane

This plane refers to your dreams and intuition. Considered the plane of enlightenment, it is linked to highly creative tendencies.

Causal aura plane

The outer aura plane harmonises all the other layers and is linked with life purpose.

Aura colours and shapes

Each of the seven layers of the aura is linked to the corresponding Chakras. The colours within the aura represent the energetic system, with bright and vibrant colours indicating health and dull, murky colours representing ill-health.

The colours and shape of the aura will also indicate areas of balance and imbalance.

According to Barbara Brennan in her book: Hands of Light - A Guide to Healing Through the Human Energy Field, a healthy aura is clear and strong, with a balanced and smooth vibrant shape around a person. When physically hunched over, a person will have an unbalanced shaped aura that reflects the physical position.

Excitement will cause your aura to light up like a Christmas tree, whereas anger will result in the murky coloured aura that may appear to have jagged shards of energy shooting off it.

Reading auras

Reading auras is a simple process, and in fact, anyone can learn how to see and read an aura by simply allowing themselves to do so. Remember, it may take a little practice before you see or feel anything.

Hold your hand up against a white backdrop and focus on the area on the edge of your fingers. When you focus, you will see a slight energy field around your hand. Or you can look at the outside shape of a tree against the sky and focus on it. You will notice a layer of energy around it.

See if you can watch this energy expanding outwards, beyond just the outline of your hand or of the tree.

Alternatively, you can feel your aura by rubbing your hands vigorously together and then gently pulling them away from each other. Gently begin to press them back together and then out again, feeling the shift in the energy. Where you feel the energy connecting, that is your aura.

If you really focus, you may be able to see colours. Healers read auras to analyse your energetic health. Based on the aura's colours, they guide you to what you need to work on.

How to cleanse your aura

There are several different activities you can do to cleanse your aura:

- Positive affirmations – a cleansing wash for your energetic field
- Meditation – focusing on your breath and feel the breath expand out into your aura
- Visualising yourself in a cleansing shower, with all the dark spots and murky colours being washed away
- Going for a swim in the sea or taking an Epsom salts bath
- Energy balancing and healing with an energy healer
- Laughing and relaxing, feeling your cares fall away

The aura is essential as it is the foundation for the physical body. It is directly connected with health and illness. Anything that happens in the physical body occurs in the pattern of the aura first.

The best way to heal and strengthen the vibrancy of an aura is through your emotional, mental and physical energy. A great way to do this is by understanding the body's energy centres – the Chakra system.

Chakras - The Energy Centres of the Body

Within our body, we have energy centres, often called "Meridians" or "Nadis". As part of this system, the Chakras are the areas of the highest density energy.

Chakras – which means wheel in Sanskrit – are power centres for our body. They are spinning wheels of energy located along the spine. Their purpose is to align the body, mind and soul.

The flow of energy is directly affected by our thoughts, emotions, health and state of mind. Chinese medicine believes that blockages in the energy centres create disruption and dysfunction in the body – causing illness, disease and pain.

Because of this, through the Chakras, we can identify a specific or root cause of a problem, whether physical, mental or emotional.

When our Chakras (energy centres) are balanced and in harmony, energy (qi or the life force) flows freely to raise our vibration: we are healthy, focused, vibrant and in touch with life.

When our Chakras are slow or blocked, the energy moves sluggishly or is stagnated:

- Physically it can be the cause of illness, disease and pain
- Mentally we feel cluttered, stuck or a sense of hopelessness
- Emotionally we can feel angry, depressed or detached from life
- Spiritually it can be feeling lost and disconnected

From a manifesting point, we will create more of what **we don't want at this level of energy.**

Chakra Health

Just like our arteries and blood vessels are the highways and lifeforce for our bodies (delivering oxygen, nutrition and eliminating waste), it is the same for our Chakra (aka energy) system.

Healthy arteries have smooth inner walls, allowing the blood to flow through them easily: it is the same principle for healthy energetic flow.

On the surface, our health goals are all some version of peak physical condition. Visually we see this in our skin, weight and strength. Clear focus and thinking is also feedback. We also know that our health practices contribute to our internal health, supporting the external changes we can see and desire.

The energetic/Chakra system also plays a vital role in our health as a whole, yet it is commonly overlooked when planning our health strategy.

When you break it down to its common goal, all personal development work (whether physical, spiritual or mindset) aims for optimum energetic flow.

Optimum energy flow is commonly referred to as an open or expanded state.

Blocked, Underactive or Overactive Chakras

Just like our arteries, Chakras can also get blocked (referred to as a contracted state). This means that the energy cannot flow – think of it like a kink in the hose.

A sluggish or slow Chakra is referred to as underactive.

An overactive Chakra is an energy centre operating over and above a healthy frequency level for extended periods. This is the definition of stress.

Similar to our physical ailments, our energetic body does not get clogged up on its own. The blockages are created through our actions – quite literally our karma.

The things that affect and cause blocked, underactive or overactive energy centres are:

- Trauma - physical or emotional
- Lack of physical movement
- Poor nutrition
- Lack of hydration
- Lack of sleep
- Stressful thinking
- Extended periods of lower emotional states
- Environmental factors
- Destructive health habits, such as smoking, alcohol, drugs etc.
- Living with drama

Open or Healthy Chakras

The universal health practices of quality nutrition, rest/sleep, movement, hydration and healing are the foundations of health in mind, body and spirit.

The great thing about self-awareness is knowing specifically where a blockage or contraction is within our energy centres. We can create elevated and intentional healing practices, specifically for this.

For example, for a blocked throat Chakra:

- Your meditation could include a specific mantra such as "I speak clearly and confidently"
- Wear turquoise or aquamarine blue, which is related to and supports a healthy throat Chakra
- Eat blueberries
- Focus on honest expression with yourself

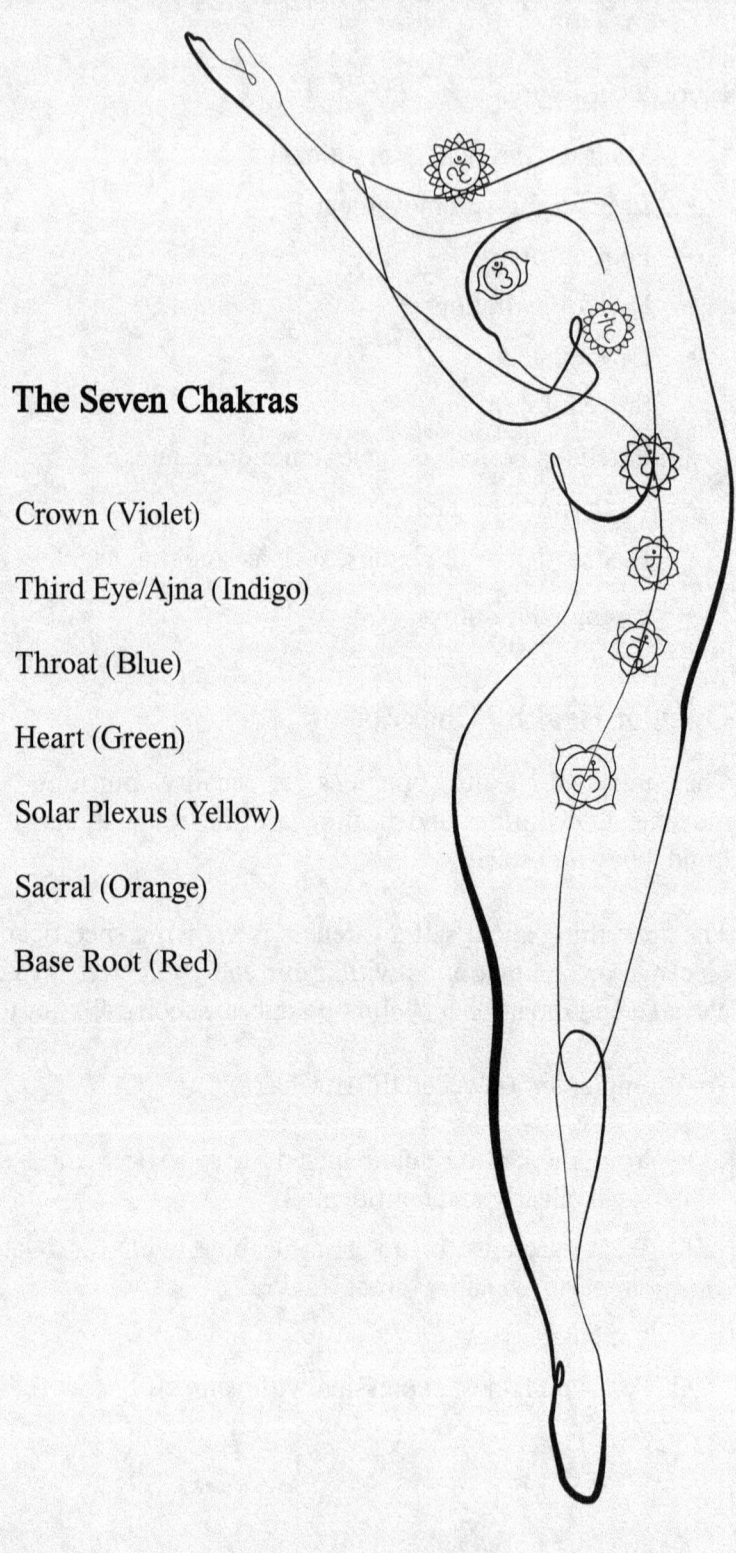

The Seven Chakras

Crown (Violet)

Third Eye/Ajna (Indigo)

Throat (Blue)

Heart (Green)

Solar Plexus (Yellow)

Sacral (Orange)

Base Root (Red)

Crown (Violet)

Location: Top of the head.

Purpose: Connection to the Universe, yourself and others – "*I understand*".

Physical: Influences the major body systems – the central nervous system, muscular and skin, memory, intelligence and focus.

Healthy (balanced and open):

- Spiritual connection (devotion)
- Inspired and creative
- Free-flowing ideas
- Intuitive knowledge
- A positive outlook on life
- Compassionate
- Grateful
- Accepting of self and others

Unhealthy (overactive/underactive, blocked):

- Unable to think beyond current situation (narrow-minded)
- Lethargic and lacking motivation
- Lack purpose
- Blame
- Lack empathy
- Judgemental
- Spiritual superiority
- Skin issues

Healing Mantra: *I belong to the Universe.*

Third Eye/Ajna (Indigo)

Location: On the forehead, between the eyebrows.

Purpose: The centre of intuition, extrasensory perception and inner wisdom – "*I see*".

Physical: It covers the pituitary gland, eyes, head and lower part of the brain.

Healthy (balanced and open):

- Clear thought
- Spiritual contemplation
- Self-reflection
- Openness
- Imagination
- Release old thought patterns and embrace the new

Unhealthy (overactive/underactive blocked):

- Unwillingness to look within
- Fear of the unknown
- Sleep disorders
- Headaches
- Nightmares
- Depression

Healing Mantra: *I am connected with the wisdom of the Universe.*

Throat (Blue)

Location: Base of the throat.

Purpose: Responsible for will, creativity, communication, self-expression and the ability to speak your personal truth – "*I speak*".

Physical: Governs the neck, throat, pharynx, thyroid, jaw, mouth, tongue, ears, neck and shoulders.

Healthy (balanced and open):

- Authentic expression comes openly and easily
- Clear and confident speech
- Healthy self-confidence
- Adaptable to change and able to listen
- Open-minded – available to others' points of view
- Healthy thyroid
- Relaxed jaw, neck and shoulders

Unhealthy (overactive/underactive or blocked):

- Neck pain
- Issues with creativity
- Self-doubt and judgement
- Problems with communication
- Trouble staying true to self
- Difficulty expressing needs and desires with self and others
- Gossiping and dominating conversations
- Difficult listening to others
- Hormone fluctuation (related to the thyroid)

Healing Mantra: *I hear the truth, I speak the truth.*

Heart (Green)

Location: Centre of the chest area.

Purpose: Unconditional love, compassion, joy, emotional power, balance. Connects the lower three Chakras (physical) to the upper three Chakras (spiritual) – "*I Love*".

Physical: The central powerhouse of the subtle body, it directly affects the heart, chest, lungs, arms and hands.

Healthy (balanced and open):

- Unconditional love
- In harmony with nature
- Harmonious relationships
- Forgiving of self and others
- Compassionate
- Non-judgemental of self or others
- Peaceful
- Calm

Unhealthy (overactive/underactive or blocked):

- Inability to love
- Judgemental
- Lack empathy
- Loneliness
- Jealousy
- Unforgiving
- Passive-aggressive

Healing Mantra: *I live in harmony with the Universe; I love life.*

Solar Plexus (Yellow)

Location: Just above the navel.

Purpose: As the centre of personal power, the solar plexus governs personality, ego and identity, as well as personal drive and will – "*I Do*".

Physical: Connected with the pancreas, organs of the digestive system and the outer adrenal glands.

Healthy (balanced and open):

- Confidence in decision-making
- Autonomy and inner drive
- Calm and flexible
- Good mood and positive thoughts
- Positive self-esteem
- Self-belief

Unhealthy (overactive/underactive or blocked):

- Fatigued and lazy
- Overeating/over-indulgence
- Feeling weak, powerless or insecure
- Manipulative, bullying or over-dominating behaviour
- Lacking self-confidence
- People pleasing and low self-esteem
- Short-tempered and gets easily offended

Healing Mantra: *I honour the power within, and I stand in my power.*

Sacral (Orange)

Location: Lower abdomen, pubic area between navel and genitals.

Purpose: It is associated with the emotional body, creativity and sensuality – "*I Feel*".

Physical: Located just below the pubic area, this Chakra governs legs, gonads, reproductive organs, lumbar plexus, kidneys and urinary system.

Healthy (balanced and open):

- Radiate warmth and playful
- Feel desirable
- Free to express yourself
- Joy and bliss in relationships
- Healthy sex life and confident in seeking pleasure
- Healthy immune system

Unhealthy (overactive/underactive or blocked):

- Guilt about sex
- Confusion with feelings
- Excessive emotions
- Obsessive behaviour
- Emotional dependency
- Kidney troubles or urinary problems
- Back pain
- Issues with reproductive organs

Healing Mantra: *I enjoy and appreciate all the experiences in life.*

Base/Root (Red)

Location: Lowest base of the spine (first three vertebrae near the coccyx).

Purpose: This Chakra supports the basic needs responsible for safety and survival. It is also the Chakra that grounds our energy – "*I Am*".

Physical: It controls the functioning of the skeleton, bones, kidneys, colon, adrenal glands, bladder, and also arterial blood flow to the left chamber of the heart.

Healthy (balanced and open):

- Responsible
- Feeling grounded
- Vitality and passion for life
- Fearless, feel safe and secure
- Desire to discover life's purpose and success
- Generates flow of energy to all other Chakras

Unhealthy (unbalanced or blocked):

- Greedy
- Insecure
- Self-centred and possessive
- Rigid, inflexible thinking and behaviour
- Overconfidence
- Short-tempered
- Depressed and withdrawn
- Feeling abandoned and ungrounded

Healing Mantra: *I am completely supported in all ways.*

Healing Modalities

There are many ways to support and heal ourselves. This chapter includes some of my favourite healing modalities, including those that aided my healing and growth.

Some are a part of my everyday routine (for example meditation, gratitude), some are weekly (Ajna Tibetan Healing), fortnightly (chiropractor) and the others are on an as-needed basis. Regardless of how often I do each one, I consider them a valuable and sacred investment in my wellbeing – I do not consider them a luxury.

It is worth noting that whether it be due to my budget or knowledge, these practices were gradually added over the years. What I'm saying is that you don't have to expect to go from one to 100 overnight with these practices, not just from the time or financial aspect, but so you can experience the benefits of each.

I encourage you to explore each one mentioned and any other modalities that may not be listed here – this list is by no means comprehensive. Make a note of your physical, mental and emotional response in the short and long term, and embrace the practices that work for you.

You just never know where each one may lead you.

For example, I found the Ajna Tibetan Healing to be of such benefit that I undertook the training to become a practitioner.

Ajna Tibetan Healing

What it is

A thousands-of-years-old healing method originating in the Tibetan Mystery School, Ajna Tibetan Healing is a powerful healing method that enables the healed person to transcend the physical.

It involves aura balancing but goes far beyond, incorporating hands-on healing and acupressure on specific body points to stimulate energy flow and release old mental, emotional and physical blockages.

How it works

Ajna Tibetan Healing differs from other healing methods by working with specific symbols and movements to tap directly into Universal energy and channel this energy to accelerate the body's own healing ability.

During an Ajna Tibetan Healing, the practitioner uses hands-on healing to balance the aura and to help release energetic blockages. These specialised movements will stimulate the flow of energy, promoting greater wellbeing, harmony and vitality.

Source: International College of Meditation & Healing
www.icmh.com.au

Reiki

What it is

Reiki has its origins in Japan and means Universal Life Energy "rei" (universal) and "ki" (life energy).

Rediscovered by Mikao Usui in the 1800s, it uses symbols and the transference of energy through the practitioner's hands to treat mental, emotional and physical disease.

How it works

Hands are placed just off the body or lightly touching the body, as in "laying on of hands". Like Ajna, Reiki healing can also be done remotely or by distance.

Kinesiology

What it is

Kinesiology is "the study of movement" with the premise that your body already knows what it needs for optimal wellbeing.

How it works

Each muscle group is related to a body part – for example, the digestive system, nervous system, and organs (linked to the Chakras).

Kinesiology uses muscle monitoring (biofeedback) to understand what may be causing imbalances in the body and how best to address the imbalance.

Acupuncture

What it is

With its roots in Traditional Chinese Medicine, acupuncture treats various conditions by using needles to trigger specific, nerve-rich points on the skin connected to multiple functions of the body.

How it works

Minimally invasive and relatively painless, insertion of the needle creates a slight injury at the insertion point, which encourages the body to respond, stimulating the immune system, leading to increased energy flow and healing.

Cupping

What it is

Originating in China, cupping involves placing cups on the skin to create suction and promoting the flow of energy. The suction can be made using heat or squeezing the cup before placing it against the skin, causing a vacuum suction.

How it works

The cups are placed strategically on the body for suction to increase blood circulation and create new blood vessels around the area. To relieve muscle tension, improve overall blood flow, promote cell repair and help form new connective tissues.

Emotional Freedom Technique

What it is

Emotional Freedom Technique (EFT), also known as 'Tapping', is a form of acupressure psychology.

How it works

EFT is based on traditional acupuncture and works with the meridians in the body. It involves gently tapping the fingertips on the skin where the energy meridians are located, diffusing negative statements and replacing them with positive ones.

Coaching

What it is

Coaching is future focused to help you grow, develop and reach your full potential.

How it works

Coaching tends to be a time bound arrangement, with a set structure and predetermined outcomes. It is often focused on developing in a particular area or a specific skill.

Counselling

What it is

Counselling is a type of "talk therapy" which focuses on working through personal challenges and past traumas.

How it works

Through talking with a trained professional, problems can be addressed in a constructive way to understand the issues, consider options, develop strategies and become more self aware.

Chiropractic

What it is

Chiropractors focus on biomechanics and the diagnosis, correction and prevention of the musculoskeletal system, specifically the spine. They believe that the structure of the spine and how it functions impacts the musculoskeletal, neurological system and blood flow.

How it works

Practitioners find and correct the maligned spinal segment(s) using joint manipulation, muscle massage, and tissue massage. Releasing previously impaired flow of energy through the nervous system is unblocked.

Osteopathy

What it is

Using a technique that includes a combination of massage, the manipulation of muscles, joints, ligaments and tendons, osteopaths focus on the whole body. Believing that the body can heal itself when it is brought back to alignment.

How it works

Osteopaths use their hands to gently apply manual therapy to reduce symptoms and improve function.

Physiotherapy

What it is

Physiotherapy restores, maintains and enhances mobility, function, wellbeing, can assist with physical rehabilitation, injury prevention, and health and fitness.

How it works

Physiotherapists use manual therapy, exercise, and education to improve the range of movement, reduce pain and stiffness, and speed up the healing process.

Massage

What it is

Through the manipulation of the soft tissue, massage relaxes the body, increasing the flow of blood and oxygen and reducing pain.

How it works

Massage is hands-on and involves rubbing and placing pressure on muscles, connective tissues, tendons and ligaments.

Yoga

What it is

Originating in India over 5000 years ago, yoga is a mind-body practice that combines strengthening and stretching poses with deep breathing, meditation or relaxation.

How it works

Originally designed to help master the mind, control the emotions and grow spiritually, yoga maintains that Chakras are centre points of energy, thoughts, and feelings. The physical movements of yoga are designed to stimulate the flow of energy.

Pilates

What it is

Developed in the early 20th century by Joseph Pilates, pilates is an exercise system that involves low-impact flexibility and muscular strength and endurance movements. It focuses on correct postural alignment, core strength and muscle balance.

How it works

A Pilates routine generally includes exercises that promote core strength and stability, muscle control, and endurance. It can be done using a Reformer machine, or on a floor mat.

Qigong

What it is

Qigong originates from China. Like yoga, it is a whole system involving the body, mind and posture, using movement to unblock stagnant energy and allowing it to flow more freely.

How it works

Focusing on the breath and using a series of gentle movements, Qigong can improve your balance and increase your strength and fitness when practiced regularly.

Reflexology

What it is

Reflexology is a type of massage that involves applying pressure to specific areas on the feet (or the hands) to stimulate the nervous system.

How it works

Along with the same principles of acupuncture, reflexology releases tension and blockages, stimulating the body's natural healing response.

Flotation Tank

What it is

A floatation tank is filled with highly concentrated Epsom salt water heated to skin temperature, with no light and no sound. Also known as sensory deprivation, it is designed for relaxation, revitalising mind and body through a meditative state.

How it works

Floating is achieved by adding a high concentration of Epsom salts to the warm water, which increases water density and buoyancy. As Epsom salts are rich in magnesium, in addition to the relaxation benefits of floating, it helps with lymph drainage, stress relief and easing aches and pains.

Journalling

What it is

Journalling is writing therapy and can be used to move into a state of gratitude. It can be used to process thoughts and feelings resulting from an event or another healing practice (i.e. meditation). Journalling is an excellent tool for future scripting, as well as a forgiveness practice.

However you use your journal, there is a similar underlying purpose of releasing and letting go of looping thoughts and emotions which clutter the mind and act like an anchor to the state of "stuckness".

How it works

It works by acknowledging the thoughts and processing the feelings around them. We can release the trapped emotions from our body and mind, gaining greater understanding and awareness.

Meditation

What it is

Meditation is primarily the practise of stillness, with a focus on the breath. There are many variations of this practice ranging from complete stillness to gentle movement. Meditation is not about stopping your thoughts, it is about stopping your thoughts from controlling you.

How it works

By bringing attention to the breath, meditation calms the nervous system, slows the brain waves and creates harmony. In effect, meditation teaches people to slow down or pause to focus inward and into awareness of the present moment.

What is Mindset/Heartset?

Mindset is the psychology of thinking.

Heartset is the psychology of emotion.

The metaphysical and biological connection and power come into play when your mindset and heartset are healthy, aligned and in harmony. Also referred to as emotional intelligence.

The disconnection between these two happens when a person is driven by their emotions (emotionally reactive) or disconnected from their emotions (apathetic or emotionally dead).

Re-aligning a disconnected and unhealthy mindset and heartset is achieved through self-love.

Assessing Where you are with Self-love

The quickest way to check-in with where you are on the scale of self-love is to look at your thoughts, behaviours and dominating emotions. If your daily habits and behaviours are part of an unhealthy lifestyle, this is a lack of self-love through a lack of self-care.

If your thoughts are limited and fixed, and your reactions are easily triggered with unbridled emotions, this is a lack of self-love through a lack of self-respect.

Self-love Practices

Self-love is having a high regard for your own wellbeing and happiness.

This is achieved through the act of doing the things that we avoid doing, are uncomfortable doing, yet stretch and feed us in our growth and confidence.

> *"The greatest act of self-love is self-discipline."*
> ~ unknown

Doing acts of self-love until they become an ingrained part of daily habits and rituals improves:

- Nutrition
- Hydration
- Rest
- Play
- Movement
- Growth and self-development work
- Caring for others

Acts of Service and Kindness

"It is one of the most beautiful compensations of life that no man can sincerely try to help another without helping himself."

~ Ralph Waldo Emerson

When we consider that the world and our external environment is a mirror, acts of kindness and caring for others without expectation are acts of self-love.

It is worth noting that this only balances as an act of self-love when there is an even balance of caring and kindness for others as there is for self. When imbalanced, it can be a sneaky way of ignoring one's own needs.

When done without attachment or expectation, these acts energise and uplift our own energy and sense of wellbeing.

Just remember that should you find yourself doing it to feel good or for someone to acknowledge or appreciate you, you are coming at it from a level of expectation. The true gift is undertaking this from a neutral stance, with care and a genuine desire to help.

Ultimately what acts of kindness and service are, is a way of paying things forward.

Aim for three small acts of kindness or helpfulness each day. This can be a simple act of smiling at someone or paying someone a compliment while standing in line for coffee. It can also be asking if a friend needs help with a task or preparing a meal for a busy family.

Students in The Happiness Hunter programs task and track three acts of kindness and care each day. We do this to make it an intentional action for each day until it becomes who we are and what we do without even thinking about it.

Remember, it is when undertaken without attachment or expectation that the ripple effect is activated.

Self-talk

Self-love is meeting yourself where you are at – without judgement. Knowing that where you are at is perfect and part of your journey. Your thoughts and self-talk are kind and from a place of compassion, love and respect.

An easy start to this is through affirmations, prayers and mantras with a theme of love, respect and nurturing:

- I am love, loved and loving
- I am worthy
- I am fully supported in all the ways

At its core, self-love is about the intimate relationship one has with self, with no requirement for external validation.

You can speak or journal these affirmations.

Being Generous

Being generous is about giving, tapping into the universal flow of abundance. Whether through your time, your money, your energy, your skills. Generosity is not self-serving and requires nothing in return. Being generous gives you something so much more: it contributes to the betterment or happiness of something or someone beyond you, making you feel good, in a way that nothing else can.

True generosity needs no acknowledgement and no applause. You don't need to tell anybody about what you did. Being generous is an incredibly overlooked and undervalued currency. The reward is in how good it makes you feel to do something good, selflessly, for another. In its truest form, being generous opens you up to receiving.

> *"That's what I consider true generosity: You give your all and yet you always feel as if it costs you nothing."*
>
> ~ Simone de Beauvoir

Journal reflection questions

Write and list at least 10 action responses to each question below:

- How can I best show up in the world today?
- How can I be of the greatest service?
- What is the greatest act of self-love that I will do today?

Attitude is Everything

Your attitude is everything. It is the foundation of what you create.

It is the way you think or feel about yourself, someone, or something, which is often reflected in your behaviour towards that person or situation.

Your attitude is a decision.

For example:

- If you have woken up on the wrong side of the bed, make the decision to go back to bed and wake up on the right side.
- If something or someone made you feel bad, recognise the decision you made to take it on, and know that you have the power to make a different decision.

A negative attitude is potentially destructive and has the power to create more of what we don't want.

A positive attitude expands our thinking and ability to receive and experience all the beauty life offers.

Self-assessment

A quick self-check assessment of your attitude is to journal your thoughts, feelings and behaviours around the following:

- Self-love
- Prosperity
- Commitment – level of commitment to follow through
- Belief – possibility
- Play
- Relationships with significant others
- Self-sabotage

Another way to assess your attitude is to check-in with the results you are currently experiencing in life.

Shifting from a Bad Attitude

Shifting out of a bad attitude is actually a simple process. The challenge is facing the level of commitment we have to the problem.

> **Step 1:** With all love and due respect, get over yourself – a bad attitude is actually making it all about you; it is a destructive, self-serving energy.
>
> **Step 2:** Make the decision to reset and show up with an empowered attitude.

It really is that simple.

Where I am now is where I am now, and where I am now is perfect.

Visualisation Exercise

Close your eyes and take in a deep breath, releasing it slowly and emptying your lungs of all the air. Repeat three times.

Visualise a ball of bright light above your head.

See and feel the rays of light cascading down from this ball over and through you, washing away the negative thoughts, feelings and energy.

Receive and allow the light to wash over you until you feel energised, focused and fully recharged.

A sign of being fully recharged and energised is when you feel an involuntary smile.

Prayer for a Positive and Energised Attitude

For today, may my spirit shine bright

For today, may I be lifted higher

For today, may I radiate positive energy

For today, may my passion be felt

For today, may I be the best of who I am

Thank you for always guiding my path and lighting the way

Thank you for always being with me

Consistency is key

> *"Small disciplines repeated with consistency every day lead to great achievements gained slowly over time."*
> ~ John C. Maxwell

Having the tools, practices, knowledge, and awareness is nothing without understanding and action. We must commit to implementation of what we know and understand. Consistency is the key to momentum and desired results.

Consistency in your action forms new habits and routines, which helps to build momentum, creating and embedding sustainable change. This action then builds upon itself in a positive upwards cycle.

By being consistent, it means you are doing what's required today to achieve the kind of life you'd like to be living. Consistency is about repetition. It is about persistence. It is about doing the same things repeatedly over time to reach the desired outcome – whether you feel like doing them or not.

Beyond the attainment of your goals, the benefits of being consistent are:

- Discipline and self-control
- Confidence
- Self-trust – our actions match our words
- Fast-tracking success and results
- Creating unexpected and welcome opportunities

Celebrating your way to Success

"Happiness is to be found in overcoming obstacles and challenges in our lives, not in the absence of them."

~ Fiona Redding, The Happiness Hunter

Every journey has an element of excitement and nervous energy at the beginning, a celebration at the end, and at times a very (very) messy middle.

It is within the mess that the magic and growth happens. It is where resilience, tenacity and confidence are forged. So for all of the discomfort it may present, the mess also offers many moments worth celebrating.

Showing up to start and undertake a task is a party and celebration worth taking a moment for. Because let's face it, when we hit rock bottom and are unhappy, it is because we stopped showing up for ourselves. The negative self-talk, limiting beliefs and the uncomfortable emotions holding us hostage in our stuck-ness are simply a by-product of not showing up.

I showed up for me today. I gave it my best. I am proud of this.

Suppose you really want to exponentially multiply the happiness of reaching a goal. The key to this is celebrating every moment and achievement, challenge faced and overcome. No matter how small, or seemingly insignificant. Everything is worth celebrating.

Remember, happiness is not waiting for you at your destination – you decide to be happy along the way.

You bring the energy and the value to the table by being you and showing up as who you are. When you truly know your inherent worth and value, the world will reflect that back to you.

Ways to celebrate

- Pause to acknowledge yourself for showing up every day and every moment for this outcome.

- Share the good news with a friend, support crew or loved one.

- Anchor the feeling of success for achieving a milestone or hearing some great news with repeated action, an affirmation or phrase.

- Anchor yourself in the moment, become aware of where you are, what you are wearing, how you are feeling. Close your eyes, feel your feet deeply grounded into the earth as you allow yourself to feel into the joy and excitement of the moment. Own this as your new reality.

- Look in the mirror and say "well done you".

- At the end of the day, journal three to five things that you followed through on to move you closer towards your goals, mission and purpose.

- Reflect on what worked really well for you today.

Remember to celebrate, no matter how big or small the achievement. Celebration is gratitude with a party.

The Emergency Fix

Doing the inner work does not mean that life's little challenges won't show up. That is wishful thinking that is only going to set you up for failure. Thinking you should know better doesn't help either. The trick here is to have an in-case-of-emergency plan to refer to when the seas get rough.

This is your lifesaver, a buoy to keep your head above water. This is an emergency life raft that can be used at any time, for any event, in any circumstances.

We all have moments and experiences where all of our knowledge, self emotional regulation and wisdom gets thrown out the window, and our emotional reactions take over. Think of a toddler in a full-blown tantrum where not even their favourite toy or food is enough to distract them from the emotion.

Subjective Units of Disturbance Scale

In psychology, to measure the subjective intensity of distress or disturbance experienced by an individual is referred to as the Subjective Units of Disturbance Scale (SUDS). SUDS is a self-measuring assessment developed by Joseph Wolpe using a scale of zero to 10 to rate the level of emotional disturbance.

The benefits of becoming familiar with this scale (you don't need to know it verbatim) is that it provides an instant self-assessment reference to where you are at, in the present moment. Because the thing with emotions is that if you can name it, you can change it – this is acknowledgement and awareness.

Using the scale and knowing where you are will allow you to pause and take action to process and ease the level of distress.

Personally, I would recommend taking action on self-assessments rated at two or above. Our emotions are the strongest indicator we have to what is going on within us, and for what we are creating, and the feelings at two are an early warning system that something needs to be addressed.

Getting to seven is at the level of losing control and you are most likely to do or say things you may regret.

This is a great tool to also have in conversing and understanding where someone else may be regarding their emotional state. For example, if someone is hitting a six or above, they get to an emotional threshold beyond logical reasoning.

As an example, you could not (and should not) introduce this tool when someone is at a seven – doing so will only aggravate the situation.

10 = Feeling very, very bad, the most distressed you have ever felt. No-one could ever imagine the anguish and torment you feel. Unable to function.

9 = Feeling extremely anxious and desperate. Highly freaked out to the point that you can't cope. On the edge of losing control of your emotions.

8 = Worried, panicking, freaking out. Losing focus and feeling physically anxious.

7 = Feeling very uncomfortable. Difficulty in functioning normally.

6 = Feeling moderate to strong discomfort.

5 = Feeling upset and uncomfortable. Still functioning, but it requires some effort to manage difficult feelings.

4 = Feeling mildly to moderately upset and worried. Managing okay but you don't feel good.

3 = Mildly upset. but still functioning. You are aware of being worried.

2 = A little bit upset or distressed, noticeable only if you pay attention to your feelings and realise that something is bothering you.

1 = No distress and generally feeling good.

0 = Peace, serenity, total calm.

In Case of Emergency...

Despite what we know, let's face it, moments happen in which we become emotionally reactive – slaves to our thoughts and feelings.

- You are about to lose it, you are losing it, you've lost it
- Yelling or screaming back at another in an argument
- A stream of verbal insults
- Thoughts, intention and action to physically lash out
- Uncontrollable crying

Basically, any action or verbiage resulting from emotion or feeling is an emotional reaction, often a sign of distress and loss of logical reasoning.

The power of the pause

Step one at any level (and especially in distress) is to simply stop. To stop talking, to stop answering back, to stop all physical activity. Just stop – create a pause.

Unless you are in physical danger, remember that walking away may only aggravate a situation further, even if you have stopped fighting back.

Suppose your situation is in an argument with another. In this particular case, your role here is to stop talking. Stop answering back, stop trying to control the situation, and allow the other person to process what they are going through.

Remember the *"I Am Teflon"* affirmation.

This is where you decide that their words and thoughts can just slide off you while you give yourself the space to respond rather than just react.

Should you stop talking or need to walk away for a few minutes, remember to communicate that to the other party to let them know that you need to settle for a moment and will return.

Sudden silence can be received as stonewalling, which can aggravate the situation further, as will walking away without communication, or hanging up the phone.

Breathe...

Centre yourself through your breath.

A fast and straightforward technique is to breathe in for four seconds, hold for four seconds, release the breath for four seconds. Then repeat and aim to do it all again to a count of five seconds. It is an excellent practice to have a go-to breathing technique for emotional emergencies.

Review

What is the best and healthiest outcome for all involved in this situation?

The answer you are looking for here is the next best move for all involved (it does not have to solve bigger or deeper issues). This could be as simple as coming to an agreement to pause and calm down and revisit at a different time.

It could be a self-reflection and assessment of the bigger picture here. Is winning this argument going to do bigger, irreversible damage to the relationship – to win the battle but lose the war? In this situation, the best outcome may be to let go or concede but remember, this is about genuinely letting go – it ends here.

However, if any of the following match your response or current emotion to this question:

- Need to be proven right – hint: you are still talking back or have a desperate need to keep talking
- Want to lash out or hurt, or make someone suffer (whether through thoughts, words or actions)
- Continue arguing
- Have elevated emotions: at them, yourself or the situation
- Cannot stop crying
- Cannot think straight

Go back to step two, continue to breathe, but extend the count period until breathing becomes more important than your focus on the current situation.

Respond

Always respond from a place of love, dignity and respect.

You will know you are ready to respond when you can think of the situation without elevated emotions.

If you are still feeling emotional, your best response is to create some space to process and come back to communicate – this is not the time to explain your feelings.

A suggested communication prompt if still feeling emotional:

> *"I am triggered right now and feeling emotional (or I'm not sure how I am feeling at all at the moment). This is not about you. I just need some space to process what is going on within me so that I can come back and communicate calmly."*

The key to this communication is removing any blame from either party. Let the other person know that you are not just walking away by ignoring or stonewalling them. But you are creating a safe space where you can both come back together to continue the discussion if that is what all parties want.

Remember...

Ultimately, your goal is to avoid ever getting to this place. But we all know that life does happen, and this is why it is essential to have a plan to course-correct when the proverbial hits the fan.

Tools and Resources

Activity: The Mind Dump

> *"The impediment to action advances action.
> What stands in the way becomes the way".*
>
> ~ Marcus Aurelius

This is a journal activity designed to do what the title says – a mind dump. It is a great place to start to help transform any area of your life.

The objective of this exercise is to create a free-flowing, decluttering of the mind. The mere act of answering the questions and writing down your thoughts will start to clean, clear and organise your mind.

The rule – write freely. No filtering, no self-editing, just writing. No matter how ridiculous the words seem, simply get it out of your head and onto paper.

Work your way through and answer each question.

Question: What is not working in my life right now?

List everything that you can think of – minor, major and everything in between. Do this for each of these areas:

- Health and fitness – nutrition, exercise and hydration
- Mindset – mental, emotional and spiritual wellbeing
- Relationships – intimate, family and friendships
- Professional/Business – career and business relationships
- Play and fun – rest, recovery and recharging
- Productivity – time, efficiency and effectiveness
- Goals – life purpose, mission and vision
- Finances – relationship with money: income, debt, spending habits, savings, wealth creation

Once you have completed your answers, go back through your list and rate the level of each problem using the colour chart below.

Green: A minor discomfort and inconvenience.

Orange Warning Sign: It can get out of control if I do not do something about it. At the moment, I am managing to live with it.

Red Alert: It is a hot mess, a significant problem, wholly unsustainable and affecting other areas of my life.

Question: What do I want?

Corresponding to everything you listed in your responses above, write down an answer for what you want. Go for gold. Do not hold yourself back or limit yourself in any way.

Question: What is stopping me from getting what I want?

Write down the first thoughts and feelings that come to mind, no matter how ridiculous it might sound. What is stopping you from getting what you want.

Question: What am I happy with? What is going really well in my life?

Review the list and make a note of what is working well for you.

Question: Do I want to continue to build on this ?

Do you want more of this, and what would it look like?

Question: How would you describe your relationship with...?

Food	Your Body	Social Life
Money	Work/Career	Time
Sleep	Family	Fun and Play

Do not self-edit or downplay it. There are no limits. If you could have any relationship, what would it look and feel like?

Meditation

After any speaking event or workshop, the most common question I'm asked is: "Where do I start to create the change?"

My answer is always the same. Start with meditation.

I recommend this as the first place to start because the first hurdle my students want to overcome is to pause, quieten, and make peace with the internal chatter (often referred to as the monkey mind).

Even though they know that they can do and be more, there is an internal dialogue that anchors them in what they don't want or want to leave behind, and they don't know how to change it.

Meditation does this, and so much more.

The key to unlocking our potential is meditation. It teaches us to listen to our inner voice, to tap into and harness the power within.

It is the way. There is no other way.

Meditation had such a profound impact on my life that I wrote my first book, The Happiness Hunter's Guide to Meditation, to help others gain the confidence to begin their own life-changing meditation practice.

What is meditation?

Meditation is the practice of centering your thoughts and consciousness into the now (the present moment). It can be practiced in stillness (sitting or lying down in one spot) or actively through a repetitive task.

The objective is to become aware and comfortable with your thoughts; it is often incorrectly assumed that meditation is about stopping or controlling your thoughts.

The most essential components of meditation are

Breath - Controlled breathing through different techniques is the quickest way to ease the mind and relax the body.

Acceptance - Allowing the thoughts to flow from a place of detached observation.

Intentional practice - A powerful step to include in any practice (including sitting down to work) is to set an intention or an objective for what you want to get from it or how you want to feel at its end.

For example, in meditation, it could be: I want to feel calmer.

Showing up consistently - Successful meditation practice is simply about showing up.

How to meditate

Find a space and time to sit or lie down. Start with five or 10 minutes. Set your timer.

Spine straight with arms by your side or hands resting in your lap. Feet flat on the floor - Close your eyes.

To a count of four, breathe in deeply through your nose. Take the breath as far down into your diaphragm as you can.

To the count of four, release the breath through your mouth - Repeat.

Breathe through any feelings of discomfort or physical tension in your body.

Observe and allow the flow of thoughts without chasing, judging or engaging in the thought dialogue. Let the thoughts come and go without attachment.

For a beginner struggling to focus, you can start the meditation with a mantra to help you focus (for example OM), or follow a guided meditation recording.

Guided meditation recordings are popular for practices of manifesting, healing, auto-suggestion and subliminal thought training.

It is recommended to have a daily meditation practice. Making it a part of your morning routine can really set your day up for success. Twice a day, even better. However, for those overcoming stress or anxiety, several short practices throughout the day will serve best.

As you advance in your meditation practice, this may happen automatically, or you will be guided by the practice itself.

> *"You should sit in meditation for twenty minutes every day – unless you're too busy; then you should sit for an hour."*
>
> ~ Zen Proverb

Recording your personal guided meditation

Here are three guided meditation scripts *(inner peace and calm, health and wellbeing, abundance and prosperity)*.

On your phone's recording app, record yourself reading through the meditation script, using a calm and even tone. Speak slowly, pausing between sentences and leaving plenty of quiet space to extend the meditation to your desired length.

Give yourself 10 to 30 seconds between each sentence. You may like to have some relaxing meditation music playing in the background as you record.

Listen to this during your meditation practice. The benefit of doing it this way is that your mind is hearing your voice, therefore more likely to accept the words.

Meditation Scripts

Select one of the following three scripts, find a quiet space and set your intention for the practice and beyond. These meditations are written with the intention of you creating a personal recording.

When you want to listen to your recording to undertake the meditation practice, sit or lie in a comfortable position, giving yourself permission to relax and unwind for the duration.

Meditation for Inner Peace and Calm

Close your eyes - Notice your breathing.

As we begin this meditation, repeat the following three times:

> I give thanks for the joy of living and being alive.
> I am calm and at peace.
>
> I give thanks for the joy of living and being alive.
> I am calm and at peace.
>
> I give thanks for the joy of living and being alive.
> I am calm and at peace.

Now turn your attention to your breath.

Listen to the sound of your breath flowing softly and gently through your nose, calmly and evenly out through your mouth.

Notice the temperature of the air as it enters your nostrils and the temperature of the air as you exhale through your mouth.

Notice the flow of air through your body.

With each breath in, feel the air coming through your nose, into your lungs, bloodstream and the cells of your body, through your organs, your muscles and into your brain.

Feel that fresh air clear out the stress and tension in your body and mind.

On each out-breath, feel all the stress and tension leave your body.

On each out-breath, feel your body sinking deeper and deeper into a calm and relaxed state.

Should you catch your mind wandering, turn your focus towards your breathing to bring yourself back to the present moment.

Allow your thoughts to flow. There is no need to follow them or engage with them.

Bring yourself back to the here and now, to your breath, to the feeling of deep relaxation, inner peace and calm.

Let your thoughts be.

Keep bringing yourself back to the breath, gently in and gently out, and to the feelings of inner peace and calm.

Focus on your breath, in and out, and the feelings of calm and peace and relaxation within your body.

When you are ready, you can wiggle your toes and your legs, arms and hands, neck and shoulders, and when you are ready, you can open your eyes.

Meditation for Health and Wellbeing

This meditation is for the perfect, living, breathing system that supports your life and being alive.

Focus on the love and appreciation for yourself and your body.

Appreciate all of the wonderful things your body allows you to do, for all of the places your body can take you, for touch, for hugging, for healing, for kindness - Close your eyes.

Feel your body fully supported by the chair you are sitting on, the bed or the ground underneath your body.

Feel the connection of your skin and your body to this solid support.

Notice how it feels to be resting comfortably.

Take a moment to appreciate how it feels to be doing something so loving, caring and rewarding for yourself.

To be giving yourself this time to rest and recharge.

To pause - To slow down - To connect.

I am aware of the sensation of the clothes I wear, the feeling of the fabric and ground beneath me - I feel the flow of air against my skin.

I appreciate me and this opportunity I've taken to pause and be in such a calm, open and relaxed state.

Notice what it feels like to simply pause, to just be.

Becoming aware of my presence within my body.

My body is the vehicle through which I travel through life.

My body is beautiful - I am beautiful.

I deserve this, my wholehearted love and positive attention.

I deserve this.

I love caring for myself - I show myself I care.

My body responds beautifully to being cared for, moved and strengthened.

My mind and body thrive with healthy nourishment.

I crave healthy food and am vibrant and energetic because of it.

I desire and seek daily health practices to nurture my body, mind and spirit - My body is sacred and holy.

I treat it with love, care and respect, and in turn, it allows me to play, love and laugh fully in life.

Because I care for, nourish and hydrate my body and mind, it is a powerful, magnetic source and vessel for everything I want and desire.

I love everything my body can do for me, and it can do and create amazing things.

I allow myself to relax and fall in love with every aspect of my being.

I breathe life into my body - I breathe.

And when I am ready and fully recharged, I will open my eyes.

Meditation for Abundance and Prosperity

Close your eyes.

In this meditation, we journey to your true essence to experience the nature of who you really are and what you are really made of.

Take a few moments to focus on your breath. Feel the air coming in through your nose, feel your chest gently rising and falling on the inhale and the exhale.

Be here quietly with your breath. With the sensation of the air moving in through your nose and out through your mouth.

Be here quietly with your body, responding to the flow of air, in and out - Feeling the connection between your body and breath.

Allow your body to relax - See the thoughts in your mind begin to slow down.

If you become aware of your mind drifting, bring your awareness back to your breath - Let the thoughts come, and let the thoughts go.

Now, I want you to bring your attention to the innermost part of you.

At your core, you are limitless, timeless, unconditional love, pure peace - You are connected to the source of all of creation.

Your essence is creation.

You are the creator of everything.

Your true essence is abundance.

True abundance is overflowing goodness.

Allow yourself to feel your connection to the source of all abundance - Abundance is your true nature.

Your breath connects you with your true nature.

Your true nature is abundance.

On each breath, feel yourself sinking deeper and deeper into this feeling.

Feel the warmth of this connection.

Feel the comfort of this connection.

Feel the love of this connection.

Within you is an infinite supply.

Within you is everything you ever need or want - It already exists.

Now, I want you to see this connection within you, see this connection with the source of all creation.

Imagine a glowing ball of light within you.

White, gold and silver shimmering, dancing light.

Focus on this ball of light, see it moving within you.

As you focus on it, you become aware that this ball of light is connected with balls of light within everything and everyone around you.

Abundance is the true nature of all things.

Allow yourself to experience the feeling of abundance within you.

Imagine what you can create with this ball of infinite light and power within you.

For the next few minutes, immerse yourself in this ball of light.

Allow the energy from this ball to expand out into the rest of your body.

Feel it fill your mind with the power of its creation.

Feel the energy moving through your body and through your hands and feet.

Become aware of this beautiful light and energy expanding your heart, connecting you with the light in every living thing around you.

This light comes from an infinite source.

The source of all creation.

There is no end to the abundance of this source.

You are entirely connected with the source of light.

As you focus on your breath, and the source of all abundance, all creation within you, you feel an incredible sense of peace.

Stay here for a few moments, enjoying this feeling.

Open yourself up entirely to the flow of this abundance.

When you are ready, you can bring yourself back into the room.

Gently move your fingers and toes, shake your legs and your hands, move your head from side to side.

When you are ready, open your eyes.

Affirmations, Afformations and Mantras

To create a new life, we think differently. To think differently means we show up differently.

For some, changing the way we think is a lot easier said than done. Often it requires taking a lot of intentional practice and repetition to create new neural pathways of thought and emotional responses.

Resources and tools such as affirmations, afformations and mantras are guiding roadmaps of thought. They are easy to remember and are uplifting, as they help us have better thoughts; reminding and connecting us of who we want to show up as.

An **affirmation** is a statement for something you desired.

- I am happy and healthy
- I am very wealthy
- Money flows to me easily and effortlessly

An **afformation** is a presupposition as to why a statement is true. I first discovered afformations through the work of Noah St. John, a keynote speaker, author and coach. Afformations are effective because our minds are wired to automatically answer a question. Unlike an affirmation which is about creating a different belief system, afformations challenge our mind to find the answer.

Afformations

- What did I do to become so happy and healthy?
- How did I get to be so wealthy?
- What epic value did I provide today in exchange for ten thousand dollars, and how did it happen so easily and effortlessly?

Affirmations for Success

I am creating an amazing life

My grateful heart is a magnet for miracles

I am capable of great things and great things,
are always happening for me

I am worthy of success, and I am grateful for the success I have
already achieved. I am committed to my success.

I am surrounded by positive people who support my success

I believe in myself

I am confident in my ability to achieve my goals

I am a force for great abundance

I am filled with energy and vitality. I love my life

I am excited for the future and the possibilities that it holds

I am at peace with myself and the world around me

A *mantra* is a word or phrase that is repeated to aid concentration, specifically in meditation.

- Om
- I am calm and open
- Today is a great day

These are some of the most powerful (yet most straightforward) tools in the journey of success. And this is evident by the number of highly successful people who use them.

By writing, reading and repeating them as a thought or out loud, you intentionally guide your present moment thinking in the direction that serves you best.

Prayers

God is my highest source; for you, this could be the Universe, Spirit, Source or Mother Nature. Prayer is an open and honest connection and conversation. It is like having a direct line to the ultimate source of strength, wisdom and comfort.

Different ways to pray:

- You can pray for blessings (asking for something)
- As a source of comfort, or concerns for self or others
- Asking for guidance, strength or a solution
- You can pray for forgiveness

Prayers can be as long or as short as you need them to be. What counts is that they are spoken from the heart.

Prayer for me is talking with God about my innermost thoughts and feelings. Meditation is listening for God, aware of the presence and guidance within.

Prayer for Forgiveness

My heart is heavy; the guilt and shame, anger and blame are consuming me from within.

I have done wrong, and I am so sorry.

I am struggling to let this go. I feel like I am being eaten from within.

Please hear my prayer.

I come before You today with a humble heart.

To confess the mistakes I have made in my thoughts, deeds and where I have not acted.

Please forgive my failings.

Guide me to do better, and teach me how to learn from my mistakes.

Help me live a life that reflects Your goodness.

For You are faithful and just. Loving and compassionate.

In Your mercy, please forgive me and purify my heart. I pray that as I am forgiven, so I may forgive.

Amen

Prayer for Support

When all is dark, please show us light.

When we feel overcome by doubt, please give us faith.

When our faith is tested, please teach us to trust.

When our souls feel crushed under the weight of despair and the weight of our worries, please give us hope.

When we make mistakes, stumble and fall, please lift us up.

When we feel like we cannot go on for another moment or one more day, please give us courage.

May Your guiding light be our refuge in our times of struggle.

May the knowledge of Your presence always with us give us strength.

May I grow even stronger in Your eternal presence, knowing the strength and power of Your unconditional love.

Please comfort our hearts and mind with Your everlasting peace.

Amen

Prayer for Blessings

Thank You for everything and everyone in my life.

Thank You for all the wonder and beauty.

Thank You for the difficulties and the challenges, which are always a blessing in disguise.

Thank You for Your guidance, wisdom and counsel. Thank You for always being with me, always loving me, always guiding me, always helping me, always making sure I have all that I need. I am so grateful.

I ask that You would use me to be a blessing to others who are in need or face difficulties.

Please help me be a source of blessing for others, a channel through whom Your love and peace and joy flows out.

May my hands bless others.

May my feet be guided to places where I can be a blessing. May my words offer comfort and encouragement to all.

Please give me the wisdom and grace to be available when others are in need.

As I receive Your blessing in all of its forms – through material abundance, loving relationships, health, fulfillment in life, hope, joy and inner peace – I gratefully and gracefully extend all of my blessings to others.

Thank You for blessing me, and so that I may be a blessing to others.

Amen

Journalling

Journalling is the practice of downloading your thoughts and feelings around a particular event, person or situation, with a desire to understand and make sense of the chaos and the jumble.

A journal is different from a diary. A diary is a recording of events as they happen, whereas a journal is used to explore thoughts, feelings and ideas. There are many different types of journals: a creative journal, a dream journal, a gratitude journal, an ideas journal.

We journal after meditation to work through the thoughts and feelings brought to our awareness as a result of the reflection.

In this scenario, there is usually very little prompt needed as we write what we are thinking, eventually coming to realise that this is our way of downloading, receiving or processing information.

In the beginning, it simply feels like you are transcribing your thoughts – just know that this is perfect.

There will be times when you face a blank piece of paper, and nothing comes to mind, or you don't know where to start. For this, the rule here is to simply start writing, whatever comes to mind, even if it is "I don't know what to write…" followed by whatever thoughts or words flow.

It does not need to make sense. The objective is to connect to the flow of thoughts of the mind; to get your feelings into written words.

My one rule (this is my adaptation of morning notes from Julie Cameron's book, *The Artist's Way*) is for the student to fill three pages of journal notes (whichever way that may flow).

This may feel awkward, uncomfortable and pointless in the beginning, and that is totally normal.

The students later realise that this is the process of practising the art of journalling. When they let go of thinking of it as awkward, to trusting and embracing the process – this is when journaling delivers its results and benefits.

I like to think of journalling as having a deeply intimate conversation with the person who knows me best and as a process for tapping into my innate wisdom.

Common challenges with journaling

I don't know what to write - Just start writing and just do it.

Privacy and security

The fear that creates the most common resistance for my students is the fear of their innermost reflections being read by another. Unfortunately, this often leads to filtering their writing which dilutes the real benefit of the process.

This is a valid fear of privacy and security and needs to be addressed logically and safely.

Here is how we approach this.

If your writing and thoughts are something that you do not want anyone to see, for whatever reason, the final step of your journalling practice would be to destroy the written pages. Some students symbolically burn. You could use a shredder or simply tear the pages into many tiny pieces.

Within our practice of The Happiness Hunter, we do not go back to re-read our journal notes – there is no need to. It is through the writing and journalling process at the time that we experience the benefits of awareness and letting go.

How long does it take to work?

It is as long as it needs to and as quick as you allow it to happen.

The one thing to note here is the more you try to control the process, the more you delay any benefits.

Like everything we do, this once again comes down to holding the vision, keeping faith and trusting the process, even though you may not see or understand why.

Does it have to be handwritten?

Absolutely yes. It is said that what is written by hand is imprinted on the heart. However, if we get down to the scientific and biological level, it strengthens the body and mind connection.

In a world of texting, typing and Googling for instant answers, we have slowly diminished our fine motor skills and capacity for critical thinking, conceptual understanding, memory recall and creativity.

Decluttering

Decluttering was popularised into the mainstream through the minimalist movement and Mari Kondo's book The Life-Changing Magic of Tidying Up.

Aside from cleaning up, decluttering became a proven practice of letting go on a physical and emotional level beyond the item in question. Mari Kondo also highlighted the value of surrounding ourselves with objects and things that brought us and filled our lives with joy.

Different ways to declutter

- The physical environment (cupboards, drawers, clothes, old boxes of memories, inside of the car etc.)
- Digital and online (emails, storage, subscriptions, social media)
- Input and mental stimulation (t.v., shows, newspapers etc.)
- One in, one out rule. Rather than continuing to accumulate things, as you buy something new, something else is discarded.

Decluttering does not mean getting rid of everything potentially seen as a "bad" thing by another. For example, watching a television show can be an excellent option to wind down and relax. Likewise, for some people, watching the news (with discernment and in moderation) can allow one to keep up with world events and stay informed.

Having snacks in the pantry allows for the occasional treat. How each of these affects our lives as a positive or negative influence comes down to balance.

How to declutter

There is always the option of a big spring clean. However, most people avoid decluttering because a big spring clean often brings more chaos before the end result, and the process of looking at your "stuff" can feel incredibly overwhelming and confronting.

Another option to practice decluttering (and recommended to do after a big spring clean) is to have a daily or twice-weekly task of decluttering.

For example:

Email - you may have an inbox of 5000 emails, which can be an insurmountable task to deal with in one sitting. Including this as a daily decluttering activity is building and practising a system of dealing with your daily incoming email and then having a goal number in mind for how much you want to reduce your existing email by each day.

Making this a daily activity allows you to practice different times and formats that are efficient and support your working day. Before you know it, you will have your own system in place.

Kitchen declutter - this could be broken down into a daily task of decluttering one drawer or cupboard per day. This can continue beyond the kitchen with laundry and bathroom cabinets.

The power of the daily declutter activity is in invoking the law of incremental movement and momentum.

Decluttering is also a great way to move you from being "stuck" and to stimulate the flow of movement. Whenever I am working towards a goal, or about to launch into a new project, I always begin with a declutter of something significant – to be intentional and to focus on creating space. To not look for a surface declutter, but to move into something that involves an element of really having to dig just that little bit deeper to let go.

As a word of caution – be very careful to recognise when decluttering is being used as a procrastination strategy. For example, you have a deadline for a project and suddenly decide that it is the perfect time to clear out the garage or wardrobe.

Note also that there is a difference between the daily tidy-up (which prevents clutter from building up) and decluttering. Decluttering includes reorganising and purging.

The boyfriend in the cupboard

The physical environment in terms of what we are holding onto, and why, often tells us hidden things about ourselves that we may not have been aware of. For example, once when I was clearing out some old boxes in the cupboard, I found a box that was literally a shrine to an old relationship.

It was a strange experience to open this box and to see what I had held onto – photos, letters, I think there were even mementos from holiday travels. It was like every memory to this boyfriend was kept in this box.

Ultimately, I realised that me holding onto all of that stuff was because at some level, I was waiting for him to come back. I didn't want to let him go. As if my love was chained to this one person in the past, and letting it go was dishonouring the experience. The fact that a decade had passed did not appear to have an impact on the narrative and emotional attachment.

It was a liberating feeling to let all of that stuff go.

Vision Board

What is a vision board?

> *"Champions aren't made in the gyms. Champions are made from something they have deep inside them - a desire, a dream, a vision."*
>
> ~ Muhammad Ali

A vision board is the visual representation of your desires and aspirations for your life. They are fun to create and serve as a valuable tool to motivate and inspire you to take consistent daily action to pursue your goals and dreams.

Our minds see in images, not words.

A billion-dollar industry is built on teaching us to change our thought patterns, speech, and how to visualise our dream life into existence. Because it works.

Our focus and energy create the outcome which works for what we want and what we don't want.

Transformation in any area of our life starts with a decision, continues with a thought backed up by emotion, and followed by action.

The vision board is the visual representation of taking action, bringing together the decision, thought and feeling, and supporting it with a visual reminder.

A vision board is a talisman of sorts, created with magical properties and strengths to remind you of your vision and quest.

Examples of vision boards

- A poster with images cut from magazines, photos or online
- A vision diary with pictures and visual reminders
- A Pinterest board or Canva poster
- A screensaver
- Images on your fridge

The full power of this process is in the physical creation.

It starts with the physical board for my students, and we use screen savers, passwords, etc., as supplementary visual reminders.

It is in the act of finding the images. Then, cutting them out and bringing them together to match your vision is a process that is filled with positive emotion and energy. This is the source of its power.

Creating a physical vision board is an absolute must-do step in creating your dream life.

How to create a vision board

Step 1 - Gather your supplies

Get a large piece of paper or poster board, as well as magazines, photos, scissors, glue, coloured markers etc.

Step 2 - Set the intention

Create the environment to elevate your thoughts, emotions and energy to a miracle mindset and open to receiving. Allow yourself to feel excited. Keep in mind that you want to create a high vibe environment. The more depth to the positive emotion, the more power is within this process.

Step 3 - Select images

Browse through the magazines and photos, cutting out the images that catch your attention. The objective is to collect a stack of images. Of course, you may not use all of them.

If it catches your eye, cut it out.

Step 4 - Organise images

Group the images into themes that support your vision, for example, health, family, wealth, success.

Assemble them on the board to create a visual story.

Once you are happy and resonate with the layout, paste the images onto the board.

Step 5 - Vision board placement

Hang your vision board where you can see it every day.

Make a practice of pausing in front of it to remind and reacquaint yourself with your vision. For example, you can affirm, "I am worthy, open and ready to receive this life. And so it is done. For this or better please, for the highest good of all concerned. Thank you".

Don't hide your dreams

A common challenge is for people to feel embarrassed about displaying their vision for the life they want. Yet, the process of creating and living your life starts here. If you are ashamed or embarrassed by your vision board, how do you expect to live it?

The embarrassment fades, especially when you start to see the results. It seems silly that you would hold yourself back from abundance due to fear of what others might think about you.

Trust and faith

When you order a pizza, you know it is going to arrive. You don't sit there and question it. You trust the process. This is the key to manifestation. It is a belief that your order will be delivered, without doubt or anxious and questioning attachment. You can just get on with your day, knowing that it is on it's way.

Your job from here is to show up each day, matching the energy of your heart's desires.

Walking

I first started walking for two simple reasons: I wanted to feel better and lose weight. But, here is the funny thing, my excuses and reasons for not walking were that I felt tired, sluggish and lacked the energy – I couldn't be bothered.

Like most, it took a stick to get me moving. And that moment came when my doctor referred to me as obese. I felt sick and ashamed because I could not believe that I had allowed it to get to a point where I was referred to as obese.

Between not getting to the gym, time and financial constraints, having two little ones – walking was the easiest and most comfortable option, especially as I had a past history and reference point where walking was quickly incorporated into my life.

The benefits were almost instantaneous, namely due to elements that I had not considered as part of this equation:

Getting Outside

There is something that happens when we are moving our bodies outside in nature. When we are in nature, we go beyond what we think and really start to feel and connect to our role in being part of something bigger than us.

There is a reason beyond explanation that we feel energised by the sea or in the mountains, near a river, under trees, in the sun, wind or rain.

Movement Creates Energy and Momentum

I thought I did not have the fitness or energy levels. What surprised me was that as unmotivated and de-energised as I was, the walking exposed untapped energy within that I had not previously been aware of.

This shows that we have more to us than we think, but we need to move to access it.

Movement is the key to unlocking this energy within, and walking is a great and simple way to move.

Improved Attitude and Outlook

I expected to start feeling better from walking. That was a given. I didn't realise that in the absence of my negative attitude and bleak outlook, not only did new and inspired ideas fill this space, I felt connected with my inner guidance and intuition.

It was a magical moment in recognising the difference between an idea and intuition. Intuition presented itself as thought with absolute certainty and strength of direction. It was like receiving clear and concise advice from someone I completely trusted.

When we are disconnected or unaware of our intuition, it is still there, but it often presents as a whisper, a little voice suggesting something: making it easy to ignore or doubt its validity.

Even disconnected from our intuition, these whispers can, and often do, turn into the proverbial smack around the head to force us into action. What happens is that our survival instinct kicks in stronger, over and above the mind chatter that keeps us in doubt.

Yet once connected, we know the difference by recognising it as a solid direction and pathway forward.

These were my a-ha moments and unexpected benefits of walking. These reasons were enough to keep on walking. Sometimes a new student needs a little bit more convincing, and for that, we look to the countless studies which have proven that:

1. Walking boosts creative inspiration

A great way to become unstuck or find a new perspective on a problem or idea is to go for a walk. According to a Stanford study, a person's creative output increased by a whopping 60% when out walking.

2. Walking is good for you physically

Countless studies back up this claim – walking has been proven to lower mortality, it's good for your heart, can reduce the likelihood of developing type two diabetes, and has been proven to impact various other chronic diseases.

Walking has been shown to:

- Increase cardiovascular and pulmonary (heart and lung) fitness
- Reduce the risk of stroke and heart disease
- Strengthen bones and improve balance
- Increase muscle strength and endurance
- Reduce body fat
- Reduce physical symptoms of minor stress and anxiety
- Increase self - reported energy levels
- Improve sleep quality
- Improve cognitive performance; reduces cognitive decline amongst older people
- Increase the size of the prefrontal cortex and hippocampus, potentially beneficial for memory
- Improve management of conditions such as hypertension (high blood pressure), high cholesterol, joint and muscular pain or stiffness, and diabetes

"I've been going on the walks regularly for the last 15 months (one-two times a week), and as cheesy as it might sound – it has changed my life. The support, energy, motivation, clarity, and inspiration I have received have been priceless and nothing short of transformational – both personally and professionally.

I love this network of people, many of whom have become great friends, and I am extremely grateful to Fiona for leading us on this journey. I cannot recommend The Happiness Hunter enough – it is soooo much more than 'just a walk' or networking – it can change the way you live and the way you work."

~Happiness Hunter walker, Bev

3. Walking makes you feel good

Walking is excellent for your physical health. It also provides a powerful boost to your mental and emotional health.

All the research findings agree that walking relieves symptoms of depression and anxiety, resulting in improved quality of life.

4. Walking is a particularly accessible form of physical activity

It is low - impact, appropriate for all age groups, does not require any special equipment, you can determine your distance and pace, do it anywhere and it is free.

The Morning Success Routine Walk

The walk comes after the meditation and gratitude practice.

Let's face it, our human nature is to put off until tomorrow what we can do today, particularly if we are feeling less than inspired. This is why it becomes tempting to delay the walk. However, the not-negotiable walk is critical to a successful morning.

Decide that you are the person who moves your body and walks each morning. Make it happen.

Ideally, the goal is a minimum of 10,000 steps a day, and it is okay if you need to build up to this. The key here is to track your actions, either through an app on your phone or a Fitbit.

The Japanese Forest Bathing Theory (Shinrin-Yoku)

Research has proven that immersing oneself in nature helps relieve anxiety and depression, boosts empathy and improves cognition. Forest bathing, or Shinrin-Yoku, is about walking in nature and allowing yourself to reconnect the inner world to the outside world, taking it all in through our five senses.

For the benefits to be realised, a minimum of 20 minutes walking under a canopy of trees is recommended. An ideal goal is to do this for 10 hours each month.

Walk mindfully, and allow all of your senses to be engaged through the experience, you can literally feel yourself "bathing" in the forest. If you can't get to a forest, you can take your shoes off in a park and walk under the trees.

The Happiness Hunter Walks

The Happiness Hunter walks are group walks led by the members of The Happiness Hunter community to support our community to live our values and vision.

The walks started from a personal need and necessity to fit in exercise and connection into a single parent schedule with very little time to play. The beautiful and surprising by-product was the community, coaching and networking that it fostered.

The first walk around Albert Park Lake in Melbourne included myself and a handful of others. From the success of that, walks were introduced into several other locations around Melbourne, first with myself leading them and then with others who stepped into the role of walk leaders.

The walks extended to regional Victoria, Western Australia, South Australia and Tasmania. We have had hundreds of walkers join us over the years.

They evolved to my vision of a space for participants to meaningfully connect with other like-minded people within the local community. To get out into nature, exercise, refresh and recharge the mind, body and soul.

Walking is a core foundation of my practice and the work I do with my clients. This is because it covers movement and exercise, expands and lifts our energy and creates a fertile mind for new and fresh ideas and thoughts, to name just a few of the myriad benefits.

It is why I recommend that if walking is not already a part of your daily routine, to make it one.

If you would like to be part of a super supportive community and to have accountability, you can look up how to join an existing Happiness Hunter walk or find out how to become a walk leader.

www.thehappinesshunter.com/walks

Emotional Freedom Technique

What is it?

Emotional Freedom Technique (EFT), also known as 'Tapping', is a form of acupressure psychology.

This technique is based on traditional acupuncture and works with the meridians in the body. EFT involves gently tapping the fingertips on the skin where the energy meridians are located. Then, cycling through each of the points, diffusing negative statements that you may currently believe to be true and then a round of infusion statements or positive affirmations to replace the old negative beliefs.

It may sound complicated, but it really is quite simple. To see it in action, and for a great resource of simple tapping videos, check out EFT expert and practitioner and my favourite YouTuber, Brad Yates. He has over 1000 videos on YouTube, with 33 million views.

I had the pleasure of meeting and conversing with Brad on both the Business Addicts and The Happiness Hunter podcasts and was fortunate enough to have Brad and his wife join us for a Happiness Hunter walk during a visit to Melbourne.

> *"Rather than letting the fear of change stop us, we can tap away from the stress and discomfort and give ourselves the freedom to examine what we might be afraid of… and discover that we actually can handle the positive changes."*
>
> ~ Brad Yates

EFT helps release limiting beliefs, traumatic memories, and self-destructing habits that cause emotional blockages and suffering.

Scientific research by Dawson Church (2013) proved EFT to be effective for a wide variety of conditions, including reductions in physical pain, anxiety, emotional stress, depression, PTSD, food cravings/weight loss issues, phobias and more.

The role of the meridians

In Chinese medicine, meridians are invisible energy pathways or channels that run through our body. Our vital life energy (called Chi or Qi) is thought to flow along these meridians. Anything that disrupts this flow is said to cause illness.

If a person is under stress, especially for an extended period, the energy in the meridians can become stagnant or even reversed. This is both the cause and the effect of disharmony within.

How did it start?

EFT has grown to be a popular healing technique and therapy around the world. It was developed in the 1990s by Gary Craig from an alternative psychotherapy discovery by Dr Roger Callahan. Dr Callahan was working with a patient that suffered from an intense water phobia and used a similar Tapping technique to cure her, and EFT was tested and tried from then on.

> *"The cause of all negative emotions is a disruption in the body's energy system."*
>
> ~ Dr Roger Callahan

How does it work?

Tapping the energy meridians and vocally expressing positive affirmations works to clear the emotional blocks from the body, helping to de-stress the body and restore balance in the body and mind – essential for our general wellbeing.

EFT is ultimately about self-acceptance and self-love. Most EFT Tapping scripts will begin with the sentence "even though I (insert negative thought or emotion here), I deeply and completely love and accept myself".

Dr Linda Wilson, Happiness Hunter walk leader and author of the book Stress Made Easy says that Tapping assists us to let go of stress in the following ways:

1. Touch is an important aspect of stress relief, and in the use of Tapping, we gently touch the face and hands in a cyclical action.

2. Tone and rhythm of voice can also be used to soothe a stressed or anxious mind or body.

3. We work to acknowledge the problem and the fact that there is a solution. These opposite positional statements help to neutralise stress.

4. Tapping also adds an element of distraction and confusion to the mind as we attempt to focus on a problem and introduce stimulation in the form of Tapping at the same time.

The mind cannot focus on two things at once, and that slight scramble can loosen stress up to the point where we can 'let it go'.

5. We use the body as our access point to stress by focusing on how stress is present in our body. This awareness, the use of all of the above and the language we use is very different from a logical or purely psychological approach to stress.

Our body needs assistance, and Tapping includes a focus on the body as a way to understand our stress.

6. Tapping has been scientifically proven to lower adrenaline and cortisol stress in several published research papers. The results are quite extraordinary.

7. Awareness is key!

As we practice Tapping and releasing stress, we come back into the frontal cortex, where we have greater clarity of thought, better problem-solving ability, and a greater perspective.

All of these things also help us to rethink our situation and manage it better.

8. As our awareness increases, we can begin to take a more holistic look at the things that create stress for us and manage those symptoms and deal with many of the experiences we have from the past that act as triggers for our stress. As we unveil these experiences and tap on them, we are less triggered and manage our stress better and better over time.

How to EFT

Tapping Points

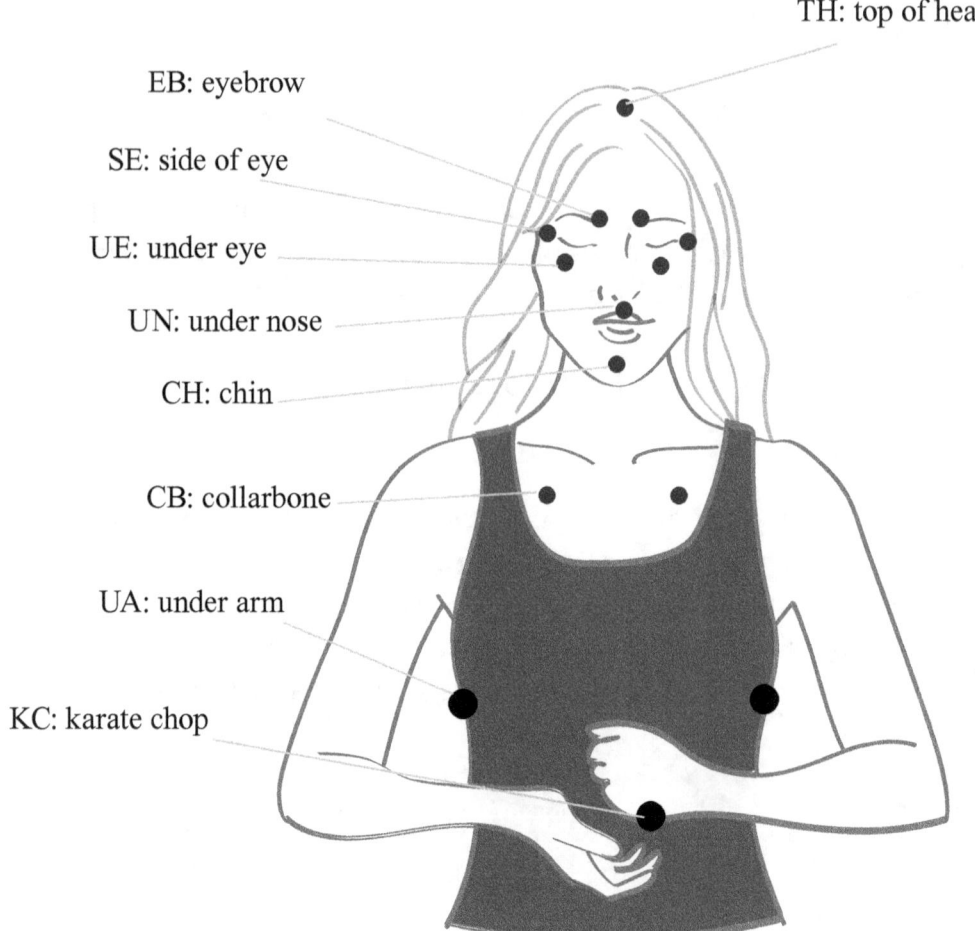

Knowing your Tapping points

The Tapping points below are listed in the order of the Tapping cycle we work through. For example, starting at position one, through to position nine and then repeating through again.

Position One - KC: Karate Chop - Small Intestine Meridian

Side of the hand: in the middle of the fleshy bit between the bottom of your little finger and your wrist, just where you'd do a karate chop.

Position Two - EB: Beginning of the Eye Brow - Bladder Meridian

Located on the edge of one of your eyebrows, just above your nose.

Position Three - SE: Side of the Eye - Gall Bladder Meridian

Located on the bone at the outer corner of your eye (not your temple, that's too far out).

Position Four - UE: Under the Eye - Stomach Meridian

Located on the bone under your eye.

Now, work your way down your face:

Position Five - UN: Under the nose - Governing Vessel

Located under the nose, above your lip.

Position Six - CH: Chin - Central Vessel

Under your lip, in the 'dent'.

Position Seven - CB: Beginning of the collarbone - Kidney Meridian

Located on the collarbone near your windpipe.

Position Eight - UA: Under the arm - Spleen Meridian

This point is in line with the nipple for men, and the bra line for women.

Position Nine - TH: Top of the Head - Governing Vessel

The part of your head that points to the ceiling.

How to Tap (EFT)

While the principles of EFT remain the same, many EFT practitioners have slightly adapted the technique.

I learned Tapping through Brad Yates and have been an avid fan and follower of his technique for years. This technique worked for me, and I know it will work for you.

In summary, EFT is the act of cycling through Tapping points whilst speaking out loud a script specific to your needs at the moment.

There are two common ways Tapping is used. The first is to use it as a tool to work through a list of challenges that are unserving beliefs, trapped emotions or trauma.

Secondly, it can be used to ease emotional distress.

In both cases, the process is the same, and the script may slightly differ.

Using the index and middle fingers of your dominant hand, lightly and continuously tap the acupressure point whilst speaking through the Tapping script.

As a beginner, you may need to read the script. Then, with regular practice, you will find your own voice and statements.

As you move through the Tapping points, know that it is normal for memories or empowering thoughts to surface. This is a normal part of the process; continue to tap through this.

Step One - Assess the emotion

Before you begin, on a scale of one to 10, assess the intensity of what you are currently feeling. Ten is the extreme of emotion, and one is the goal.

The objective is to check in between Tapping cycles to assess if the intensity of the emotion has reduced. This is measured by the number allocated to how you are feeling at that moment.

Step Two - Set the intention

To set the intention, decide the emotion and the thoughts that you want to clear. For example, you may be struggling with thoughts of not being enough, which is commonly associated with feelings of anxiety, self-doubt, sadness or anger.

In this case, your Tapping script would address the unserving thoughts, emotions and the feeling of not being enough.

Step Three - Tap through the points

Choose your script.

Tap through each of the points while reading the corresponding sentences.

Step Four - Closing out the practice

Depending on how you are feeling, there are several ways that you could close out this practice.

- Drink water

    Make this a non-negotiable as it continues to move the energy, flush and cleanse the body, as well as rehydrating (which is especially helpful if there were tears)

- Take a nap; this is highly recommended if there was a heavy or a significant release of emotion and tears

- Have an Epsom salts bath

- Get outside and go for a walk in nature

- Journal

The following Emotional Freedom Tapping (EFT) scripts can be modified to meet your specific needs.

- Tapping for stress and anxiety
- Tapping for forgiveness and healing
- Tapping for abundance

Before you start, identify the issue and the intention.

Rate the feeling around the issue a number on a scale between 0-10.

10 being the most intense and 0 as a non-issue. Go with the first number that pops into your mind (it's also helpful to write down your starting number and what you are feeling, allowing you to track your progress). It is important to recognise that this process can raise uncomfortable feelings and memories, and if your distress is too much, you might find it easier to work through this process with a professional.

Start tapping on the negative statements, feelings and thoughts which come to mind. Do not filter your thoughts as this process is what reduces the resistance, in turn creating the mental space to insert and accept the rounds with more positive statements.

Take a deep breath, taking full responsibility for your health and wellbeing, and begin tapping on the Karate Chop point (KC).

TAPPING FOR STRESS AND ANXIETY

(KC) "Even though I feel completely stressed and anxious about _____, I deeply and completely love and accept myself.

Even though this situation is so stressful, I deeply and completely love and accept myself.

Even though I have got no idea how I am going to deal with this situation, I deeply and completely love and accept myself.

Even though I can't stop thinking about it and I just want to curl up into a ball to make it go away, I deeply and completely love and accept myself.

Even though I don't really believe this tapping can work, I deeply and completely love and accept myself"

Round One

Eyebrow (EB): All of this anxiety

Side of Eye (SE): All of this stress

Under Eye (UE): All of this worry about _____

Under Nose (UN): I'm so tired of it

Chin (C): I'm so sick of it

Collar Bone (CB): Of always feeling so anxious

Under Arm (UA): Of all of this worry

Top of the head (TH): I feel so alone and scared

Take a deep breath.

Round Two

    Eyebrow (EB): I feel completely overwhelmed

    Side of Eye (SE): This stress is so debilitating

    Under Eye (UE): This situation _____ is an unbearable pressure

    Under Nose (UN): So much anxiety

    Chin (C): I feel so helpless

    Collar Bone (CB): The anxiety is never ending

    Under Arm (UA): I can feel it in my body

    Top of the head (TH): It is deeply uncomfortable

Take a deep breath. Check in with yourself. How are you feeling now? What is the intensity of the emotion on a scale of 0 - 10? The goal is we want to get you to a 0. You may find some feelings and thoughts have bubbled up to the surface, things which may have been forgotten until now - a memory, something someone said, or emotion. Write it all down. You can come back and tap through these things later.

You may find yourself sneezing, yawning, coughing or crying. You may feel discomfort. This is a perfectly normal reaction to the process of shifting stuck and stagnated energy.

Drink water to assist the process.

Round Three

    EB: So much anxiety

    SE: So much stress

    UE: So much pressure

    UN: All I want is to feel better

    CP: A sense of ease

    CB: To know what to do

    UA: But the stress

    TH: It's too much for me to bear

Take a deep breath. Check in with how you are feeling. Give it a score of intensity between 0 – 10. You will start to feel relief, it may not be felt immediately, but it will happen.

Keep tapping.

Round Four

EB: I still feel quite anxious _____

SE: But I do wonder if it is possible that I could let this go?

UE: What would it feel like to let my feelings of stress and anxiety about this go?

UN: I am open to feeling a sense of ease with this situation about _____

CP: I allow myself to imagine that I could feel calm about this

CB: I am open to that

UA: That this feeling could disappear

TH: That it could be gone right now

Round Five

EB: I already know what to do

SE: I'm safe

UE: I am completely supported

UN: How does it feel to think like that?

CP: It feels open and expansive and allowing

CB: I have the answers already within

UA: I can feel calm and confident with whatever is happening

TH: It is safe for me to let go of all of the anxiety and stress. It is safe for me to feel calm. I allow myself to feel so supported. It is safe for me to trust that I know what to do. I am completely supported. I feel calm and peaceful in body, mind and spirit.

Take a deep breath. Check within and rate the level of intensity now. Make a note of any changes to your emotions, and how you are feeling in your body. Be aware of whether the intensity has decreased, or if you are looking at it differently.

If you are still feeling an intense emotion, repeat the process, and see what else comes up for you. Ideally, you want to get to a two or below, with little or no intensity to the emotion.

TAPPING FOR FORGIVENESS AND HEALING

Tapping on the Karate Chop point (KC) "Even though what has happened is unforgivable, I deeply and completely love and accept myself.

Even though what I/they did is so terrible, I deeply and completely love and accept myself.

Even though I do not want to let this go, I deeply and completely love and accept myself.

Even though I/they deserve to be punished for what I/they did, I deeply and completely love and accept myself.

Even though I cannot ever imagine that I can forgive myself/this person/this situation, I deeply and completely love and accept myself.

Even though I don't really believe this tapping can work, I deeply and completely love and accept myself"

Round One

Eyebrow (EB): I am so angry

Side of Eye (SE): I feel so betrayed

Under Eye (UE): I feel so hurt

Under Nose (UN): I feel so let down

Chin (C): I feel so bad

Collar Bone (CB): So much anger

Under Arm (UA): So much pain

Top of the head (TH): It is so unfair

Take a deep breath.

Round Two

Eyebrow (EB): What they did

Side of Eye (SE): It is inexcusable

Under Eye (UE): So selfish

Under Nose (UN): So unkind

Chin (C): So thoughtless

Collar Bone (CB): I can feel it in my body

Under Arm (UA): The anger

Top of the head (TH): The betrayal

Take a deep breath. Check in with yourself. How are you feeling now? What is the intensity of the emotion on a scale of 0 - 10? The goal is we want to get you to a 0. You may find some feelings and thoughts have bubbled up to the surface, things which may have been forgotten until now - a memory, something someone said, or emotion. Write it all down. You can come back and tap through these things later.

You may find yourself sneezing, yawning, coughing or crying. It may be a feeling of discomfort. This is a perfectly normal reaction to the process of shifting stuck and stagnated energy.

Drink water to assist the process.

Round Three

EB: I cannot let this go

SE: They do not deserve my forgiveness

UE: They need to be punished for what they did

UN: They need to pay for the pain and suffering they caused

CP: I feel so chained to this pain

CB: I don't know what to do to let it go

UA: I don't want to forgive them

TH: I want them to suffer as I have had to suffer

Take a deep breath. Check in with how you are feeling. Give it a score of intensity between 0 – 10. You will start to feel relief, it may not be felt immediately, but it will happen. Keep tapping.

Round Four

EB: I still find it hard to let this go

SE: But I am opening to the idea that maybe I can

UE: What would happen if I forgave?

UN: If punishing them was only punishing me?

CP: I am open to releasing this anger

CB: I am open to letting go of these feelings of betrayal

UA: I am open to releasing the need to hold on to this pain

TH: I am open to letting it go, in every cell of my body

Round Five

EB: I am ready to let this go

SE: I am ready to let go of this anger

UE: I am ready to let go of this pain

UN: I am ready to release myself from the shame and judgment

CP: I allow myself to let this go

CB: I am choosing peace

UA: I can feel the relief of the letting go

TH: I forgive them for all they have done and I set myself free.

It is safe for me to let go of this pain. It is safe for me to let go of this judgment. I release myself from the attachment to the pain in body, mind and spirit

Take a deep breath. Check within and rate the level of intensity now. Make a note of any changes to your emotions, and how you are feeling in your body. Be aware of whether the intensity has decreased, or if you are looking at it differently.

If you are still feeling an intense emotion, repeat the process, and see what else comes up for you. Ideally, you want to get to a two or below, with little or no intensity to the emotion.

TAPPING FOR ABUNDANCE

Tapping on the Karate Chop point (KC) "Even though I feel so worried about money, I deeply and completely love and accept myself.

Even though I feel so scared about my finances, I deeply and completely love and accept myself.

Even though I am so angry with _____ about this situation, I deeply and completely love and accept myself.

Even though I don't know how I am going to pay _____, I deeply and completely love and accept myself.

Even though I have such a deep-seated discomfort around money and finances, I deeply and completely love and accept myself.

Even though I hate talking about and thinking about money, it's all I ever seem to be able to think about, I deeply and completely love and accept myself.

Even though I don't really believe this tapping can work, I deeply and completely love and accept myself"

Round One

   Eyebrow (EB): All this fear around money
   Side of Eye (SE): All this lack
   Under Eye (UE): All this worry
   Under Nose (UN): Never feeling like I have enough
   Chin (C): Always feeling so scared
   Collar Bone (CB): I spend so much time thinking about it
   Under Arm (UA): It causes me so much stress
   Top of the head (TH): I feel so powerless
   Take a deep breath.

Round Two

Eyebrow (EB): I just want it to end

Side of Eye (SE): These terrible feelings of not enough

Under Eye (UE): Of worry

Under Nose (UN): I don't know how I am going to pay my bills

Chin (C): I feel so anxious about the future

Collar Bone (CB): These feelings of shame around money

Under Arm (UA): Never having enough

Top of the head (TH): Feeling so exposed and unsafe

Take a deep breath. Check in with yourself. How are you feeling now? What is the intensity of the emotion on a scale of 0 - 10? The goal is we want to get you to a 0. You may find some feelings and thoughts have bubbled up to the surface, things which may have been forgotten until now - a memory, something someone said, or emotion. Write it all down. You can come back and tap through these things later.

You may find yourself sneezing, yawning, coughing or crying. You may feel discomfort. This is a perfectly normal reaction to the process of shifting stuck and stagnated energy.

Drink water to assist the process.

Round Three

    EB: Sometimes I feel like I cannot breathe

    SE: It is too much for me to worry about

    UE: It never ends

    UN: I just want it to stop

    CP: So much anger towards _____ for the position I am in

    CB: I don't know what to do to make it better

    UA: I don't know how to let it go

    TH: These feelings of powerlessness around my finances and money

Take a deep breath. Check in with how you are feeling. Give it a score of intensity between 0 – 10. You will start to feel relief, it may not be felt immediately, but it will happen. Keep tapping.

Round Four

    EB: I want to feel a sense of ease with money

    SE: To feel abundant

    UE: To see myself in the flow of abundance

    UN: Equal giving and receiving

    CP: Stepping into the feeling of universal flow

    CB: Feeling like an open and generous conduit for sending and receiving money

    UA: Allowing myself to receive

    TH: Feeling safe with money

Round Five

    EB: It is safe for me to receive, with gratitude

    SE: It is safe for me to give freely, without expectation

    UE: I am opening myself up to the flow of great abundance in all areas of my life

    UN: I am allowing myself to feel a sense of ease and flow with all aspects of money

    CP: I release myself from the pain of my past

    CB: I release all the old attachments and stories I have around money

    UA: In every cell of my body

    TH: It is safe for me to feel safe with money. It is safe for me to feel supported by money. It is safe for me to be friends with money. Money is simply an energy and I allow myself to open to the flow of the energy of money. I allow myself to feel open and expansive when I think about money. I am open to the flow of great abundance in every area of my life, in body, mind and spirit.

Take a deep breath. Check within and rate the level of intensity now. Make a note of any changes to your emotions, and how you are feeling in your body. Be aware of whether the intensity has decreased, or if you are looking at it differently.

If you are still feeling an intense emotion, repeat the process, and see what else comes up for you. Ideally, you want to get to a two or below, with little or no intensity to the emotion.

Bringing it All Together

Up to this point, I've provided you with the tools and resources I implemented or personally developed over the years in my quest for happiness. However, it's easy to forget how overwhelming this information can be for someone new to this work or just starting their journey.

Questions regularly asked are: "You decided to stop drinking - what happened next? What happened in the first days and weeks after that? What did you do? How did you deal with it?"

What messages was I giving myself to decline the drink when I really, really, really wanted it?

To bring all this information together and set you up for your next 30-days, I'm stepping back to share the beginning of my journey of giving up alcohol.

My Moment of Truth

A couple of months before I finally decided to quit for good. I was driving my car - hungover. I looked into the rear vision mirror and could see my kids sitting in their car seats. Then, as I turned my gaze forward, I caught my reflection in the mirror - my eyes looking at me and me back into them.

By this stage, for the most part, I had successfully avoided ever looking at myself in the mirror, simply because I couldn't stand the sight of myself. Yet, at that moment, I connected with something. It's not something I could explain, but it was a profoundly impactful moment.

As I looked into my eyes, I heard a voice: "Fiona, you have to stop drinking and start meditating".

Something clicked. Not only did I hear the message of what to stop doing, I knew what I had to do instead.

At the time, I had no idea where this message was coming from; all I knew was that it was a hard truth and a clear direction - I trusted that voice.

I'd had enough of the hangovers, anxiety, self-loathing, and the time spent thinking about it. I was trying to build a business and yet coming up against myself the whole time.

I knew that alcohol wasn't part of my vision and version of success.

Although I heard the message "Fiona, you need to stop drinking" previously and precursor to every failed attempt, the difference at this moment was the instruction to shift my gaze from what I didn't want (drinking) to a progressive pathway forward (meditating).

I had direction.

Drinking was initially a social lubricant, which evolved into a band-aid and eventually became a crutch - practically becoming a life-support system where I couldn't function without it.

It numbed the pain of my feelings, which were angry and depressed, and masked an underlying sense of futility. But unfortunately, while it dulled the internal chatter, it also ramped up the self-serving "poor me" dialogue.

Deep down, a part of me knew that without the "drink", I would have to face the feelings and emotions I'd spent so much time avoiding. It would mean dealing with them in full force and unfiltered.

Hence, my previous attempts were to modify, cut back or control the amount I drank because I didn't want to face any of it. I gave myself an out by trying to moderate my drinking rather than quitting with a solid cold turkey approach.

> Life-changing transformation work can be challenging and, at times, painful - it's not a journey that everybody is ready for, nor is it for the faint-hearted, because if it were - everybody would be doing it.

Recognising that there would be significant and small challenges along the way and having a simple plan of action to address these challenges was crucial and key to succeeding.

Facing my Challenges

Challenge: Habitual drinking / Drinking habits

Drinking had become an unconscious and automatic behaviour. As a result, my daily routine revolved around my next drink.

Solution: Replacing alcoholic drinks with herbal teas and soda water with a dash of lime.

I was so used to drinking something in the evening that I didn't know who I was without it, so rather than disrupt the habit, I replaced the problematic content with an alternative.

Challenge: Dealing with the void and space left without the act of drinking.

Suddenly I had a vast expanse of time in which I didn't know what to do with myself. I honestly had no idea how I would get through the day or evening without drinking in those first days. It felt like a vast barren desert of time that I didn't know how to fill.

It was intimidating and, at times, terrifying, as I had to face myself and contemplate how to fill this time, feeling so lost, purposeless and alone, thinking, "I don't know what to do."

Solution: Going to bed earlier and listening to a guided meditation. Because going to sleep without the aid of alcohol to pass out meant that I was alone with the thoughts, memories, and emotions I'd been avoiding.

Challenge: Temptations and external influences to drink.

Solution: In the early days, I avoided putting myself into challenging situations or just removed myself from them. I was going to succeed and was willing to do what I needed to do, including letting go of the things that would get in the way of my success.

For the occasions I couldn't avoid, I politely declined the offered drink or passed the glass to another person. The key here was that I was firm and resolute in my decision.

Challenge: Other people's reactions and what my abstinence from drinking meant for them.

My decision to not drink was challenging for those around me; for some, it upset the status quo of our social settings, and for others, it was the elephant in the room that nobody wanted to discuss.

I recognised that my changes could be challenging for others to accept, especially as it highlighted that I had a drinking problem and what this may have revealed with the drinking habits of my peers and social circle. I had always been the biggest drinker, often the 'last man standing', so when I wasn't that person anymore, it opened the door for others to reflect on their drinking habits.

My decision triggered others.

Solution: To empathise and recognise that my decision was not only a significant change for me, it could also affect others in a big way. To remember that their reactions were not about me or personal. It was simply that my decision and action may have triggered something within them.

Remember, the key here is EMPATHY and to know that it is not always about you.

Challenge: Communication with people who would dismiss or challenge my decision.

Responses from friends range from: "Oh, you're not so bad" (downplaying the level of the problem) to the nay-sayer of - "you're not going to stick at it… you've never succeeded before".

Solution: I learned how to talk to people and share what was going on in a way that empowered me.

Finding ways to be firm and solid in my communication without being judgemental - "no thanks, I'm not drinking". And to calmly repeat the message as often as was needed.

When people asked me if I wanted a drink, I said "*no*". Then would come the next inevitable question – how come? I had a response practised and ready: "*because it wasn't working out for me anymore*".

I communicated without making it a big deal or turning it into a drama-filled conversation. But, more importantly, I spoke without triggering the internal judgement of my past failures.

Challenge: Identity crisis

For most of my adult life, my identity revolved around being a party girl, a big drinker and being social. So who was I if I wasn't any of these things?

Solution: I got clear on who I was without drinking, who I wanted to be, what I wanted for the experience of my life, and how I would show up.

Embracing this new identity and version of me meant that I began to think, feel and act in a new way, which inevitably became a self-fulfilling prophecy.

Challenge: Loneliness, loss of community and sense of belonging.

My social scene and community had centred mainly around alcohol. Removing myself from this temptation meant spending more time on my own. Raising questions of belonging: who am I, and where do I belong.

Solution: I created a new support system and social settings.

For support, I signed up to Hello Sunday Morning (HSM) and connected with a new network of people who were also reassessing their relationship with alcohol. I committed to that, checked in every day, and made the time and effort to build relationships with a support crew who could help keep me accountable. Many of whom I am still friends with today.

Socially, I redirected get-togethers to non-alcoholic gatherings (i.e. coffee catch-up) or physically active (meeting up for a walk).

Challenge: No income to invest in help, support or a coach.

Solution: Seek out a not-for-profit support and specialist community. For me, this was HSM.

I got resourceful. There is so much information currently available to us. Books, YouTube videos, blogs, Google searches etc. - it's all out there. In addition, free support groups like Alcoholics Anonymous are available and have meetings worldwide. HSM was my choice, a free support group for those looking to reassess their relationship with alcohol.

Ask for help: It is more than okay to ask for help; you just never know what doors or support it may open.

Challenge: The inner critic self-talk of doubt or lack of confidence in my ability to succeed.

Dealing with the switch of thoughts: from spending time and energy planning to drink to obsessive and excessive thoughts of "how not to drink" or "avoid the drink".

I learned to use the negative emotions of self-loathing, shame and guilt as cues to help me overcome the beliefs that kept me stuck.

Solution: Live and operate from the present moment.

It was all about being present and caring about the Fiona of tomorrow. By wanting what was best for her, I could make the decisions today that best served her in the future.

Journalling was a crucial activity in this process to address the thoughts and feelings that were bubbling up (seeking a positive message, guidance or responses from these thoughts), using the negative as the contrast to build a more positive mindset.

I regularly reminded myself of the positive outcomes (i.e., I no longer experience hangovers). I was grateful for everything and celebrated all of my achievements.

Full participation in the HSM community, tracking, checking in and supporting other community members.

Challenge: Physical and emotional detox

I didn't realise it at the time; amongst other things, alcohol had become my sleeping aid, which created issues with falling asleep once I stopped drinking.

I experienced physical and chemical withdrawals: which led to headaches, low mood, lethargy, and irritability.

Solution: Support the detox process

Recognising this was a physical and emotional detox, I accepted the process and reminded myself that the time would pass. I drank lots of water and went on daily walks, which was the start of The Happiness Hunter group walks.

Here too, I practised the daily reminders of the positive changes - clearer skin, sparkling eyes, vastly improved energy.

Challenge: There is always a reason to drink

This social conundrum was a big hurdle to overcome, especially if I was feeling good from abstaining for the shortest time. Drinking to celebrate, to relax, wine with dinner or simply because it is the end of a stressful day are socially accepted and celebrated cues.

So, with no hangover and feeling self-virtuous and delusional about my level of self-control, it was very tempting to have one drink.

Solution: Have a clear vision of the future and not settle for anything less

I knew what I wanted and committed to the vision. Once again, it came down to reminding myself of this every day and every moment if needed. I accepted that right now was where I had to begin and repeated this each day.

In hindsight, every failed attempt was because I would prematurely declare success with overcoming problematic drinking and reward myself with a drink (oh, the irony).

The key to success was embracing long-term commitment. Then, reminding and renewing this commitment every day.

The funny thing about the tipping point of success - you will only see it in hindsight. But, it's only a tipping point because you continued to take action to support that decision.

My Framework for Getting Started

The framework presented here is what I used to give up a problematic drinking habit (something which was consuming my life and health). Yet I have used the same framework repeatedly to overcome any challenge or to meet a goal.

It is the pathway to success.

Have a big goal that aligns with the vision of a higher and better version of you

My higher vision is to be the fittest, healthiest and happiest I have ever been and be an excellent role model for my kids. To realise my fullest potential - live, be and do it through my daily choices and action.

Initially, my goal was to stop drinking; however, it didn't take long to connect it to a bigger vision and momentum to kick in.

Action: Sit down and write a clear vision and goal.

Hint: It isn't big enough if it doesn't excite you or give you nervous butterflies.

Make a decision and commit.

The first new thing I did from my previous attempts was to stop drinking 100% - not moderating, cutting back or making rules around drinking amounts and days. Unfortunately, by attempting to negotiate my drinking amounts and days, I was fooling myself into thinking I was in control.

Because, let's face it, with most of the tools and resources I've used to succeed and recommended in this book, I had previously practised them at various points along the way. But it would never succeed long term because it was all built on a half-hearted commitment.

It was a wishy-washy commitment. I had to go all in.

100% commitment was not only my guide; it pulled me up and back toward my goals when temptation struck. Or when things didn't always go as planned.

Action: Take a moment to review your decision and commitment. Be brutally honest; if you are not willing to make a 100% commitment to it and follow through on your promise - revisit what it is you want.

Have a simple action plan - preferably with external support

We often overcomplicate the simplest of things and think we can do it alone.

I kept my decision simple - "I don't want to drink anymore".

My failed previous attempts showed that I needed support and accountability; I joined Hello Sunday Morning.

The beauty about not giving up on yourself is that you can look back at the past attempts and see what could be improved. In my case, I knew the missing piece was external support and accountability.

I'm a big fan of accountability to help us achieve our goals, and there's nothing better than the support of others to help us be accountable for our promise to ourselves.

Action: Make a note of two to three simple action steps that you can take now and each day forward to move you toward your goals.

Have an attitude of success and never give up on yourself

My decision and first course of action came from an attitude of hope. However, hope can also be fragile if not partnered with an attitude of never giving up on yourself and being willing to do whatever it takes.

My early days and steps seemed to create more chaos than the clarity I sought, leading to questioning or self-doubt. Yet, it was a determined attitude that overrode any self-doubt.

I may not have known how I would do it, but I was going to do it.

Action: A reminder and affirmation for those moments when there is chaos, self-doubt or setback:

Remind yourself that it's not failure; it is simply feedback, and repeat to yourself, "I'm going to figure this out."

Clear the clutter, calm the chaos

Clearing the clutter and calming the chaos is about making space. For me, this process started as physically clearing and cleaning up my area. Then, I followed closely with mental and emotional decluttering through journalling and blogging as I talked through my experience at the time.

Something worth mentioning (especially as I want to acknowledge my younger self) is that I was intentional about how I spoke or discussed my situation and circumstances in moments of intense anger and sadness. As tempting as it was to verbally offload what I felt and thought then, I remained respectful of all involved in this situation.

Not falling prey to the toxic narrative of blaming or putting other people down cleared not only a big chunk of mental and emotional clutter and chaos in those moments - but also eliminated future clutter.

Looking at it now, I can see how my bigger vision of harmony in all relationships kept me on track.

Action: Start a daily decluttering schedule with the intention and affirmation of letting go of the good and bad to allow in the great.

It can be as simple as your immediate physical area, email inbox, to your narrative and the language that keeps you anchored in the problem.

Back yourself, by developing unshakeable faith and belief in you..

Our lives are a self-fulfilling prophecy, and what we believe, we will achieve. But, expand this unshakeable faith and connection to a higher source of power (be it God, source or the universe), and suddenly, it is like the world around us conspires for our success.

I came into this process as a non-believer in anything beyond the physical world. While my upbringing included the Anglican Church, it was something I had turned my back on many years earlier.

Yet unexplainable things started happening in my favour - beginning with that experience of the rearview mirror where I heard that voice tell me to stop drinking. After that, I began to have more of these experiences where I felt wholeheartedly guided and supported, even when things didn't make sense.

Knowing that I could do this was what started this journey. I backed myself. Connecting and tapping into a higher source of power, wisdom and guidance added a deeper level of certainty and strength.

I realised I was never alone in this journey and was unconditionally loved and supported.

Action: Take a moment each day to meditate and connect to the highest and unshakeable version of you and the source that conspires to your success.

Your Next Four Weeks

Remember: we are not chasing success or results here; we are pursuing the habits.

As you embark upon the tasks of the next four weeks, focus on fine-tuning your daily habits, declutter what is not working and re-organise your life to create the space for the change.

We start with tracking the core daily activities.

You may resist this step because it feels like too much effort, and just quietly, it can be tedious. However, tracking and measuring are the foundation of success.

It's the data you need to see where you currently are, what is working and what isn't. Sometimes it is the simplest of tweaks in our daily habits that bring on the most significant changes.

Week One: Track your activity

Download or recreate in excel the simple tracking template provided. For the first seven days of this challenge, track the following:

Sleep - with a coloured marker, colour block your sleep time (when you go to bed and wake up).

Nutrition - with a different colour, colour block the times you eat, including snacking. Anytime you put something in your mouth, colour block the time slot.

If you want to take this to the next level, you can track what you eat and your water intake on a separate sheet of paper.

With different coloured markers, colour block the following tasks:

Exercise - only log sessions 30 minutes or longer

Work - whether housework, parenting tasks or job

Social time - time spent with others but not working

The challenge is to track this data throughout the day, not at the end of the day or week (remember, it's not our memory that we want to track).

End of the week review

In the first week of tracking, we are building the habit of recording how we spend our day and then reviewing the data to see if we have consciously and unconsciously set up the patterns and rituals for ourselves.

We can then match this data with what works for and against our goals.

Sleep: Are you getting enough sleep?

Is there consistency with the times you go to be and wake up?

Remember, sleep deprivation is the quickest way to break a person's willpower and intelligent decision-making process.

Nutrition: Is there a consistency to your meal times, or is it haphazard and opportunistic?

If you are tracking what you eat, are your meals nutritious and fuel for your body? Are you drinking enough water?

Exercise: Is there enough movement and activity in your week? Is this amount on par with your goals?

Work: Take a moment to assess the level of productivity and outcomes for the week. Does the amount of time spent working or on tasks match the results?

Social Blocks and White Space: Assess the balance of social interactions (relationships and network) versus the space - time for self - is there a healthy balance?

Do your sleep hours and white space allow enough time to rest and recharge?

Remember, the week one goal is to track and review simply. By doing this exercise alone, you will adjust some of your behaviours.

If your tracking was inconsistent or you needed to backfill a day of data. Do you have many reasons (aka excuses) as to why you couldn't track or forgot to track?

Are you excited by tracking the data and how it builds the foundation of your success, or is it a chore?

If your tracking was inconsistent or incomplete, repeat this task, before moving onto week two.

Life-changing transformation doesn't happen by racing through a checklist of tasks - it happens by deliberately building a solid foundation of skills, habits and rituals.

Week Two: Adjust and track

Continue to track your daily activity as per week one.

Set an action or intention of adjusting one to two sets of behaviours for the week (with sleep being the first focus). Remember, the focus is to continue building upon the tracking habit.

Sleep: Creating a quality sleep routine will have the quickest mental and physical impact on your health.

Your goal: consistent and quality hours of sleep

For the second goal: choose a simple task. For example, if you didn't track your food the first week, you could add this into week two. Remember, it is not a diet overhaul, simply tracking of data.

Alternatively, it could be increasing water intake or including a 30-minute walk each day.

End of week review:

How consistent were you with tracking?

The underlying pattern we are looking for is how much are our goals and vision a part of our daily action (even if it is in the simplest form of tracking our daily activity).

If it still feels like a chore, your homework is to watch the original 80's movie The Karate Kid with Ralph Macchio (the underlying message here is that the simple and unassuming tasks build the foundation of strength and skill).

Did you improve the quality of your sleep routine, or was last week's pattern confirmed?

If you set a second task and goal for week two, did you achieve it?

Were there any other surprising areas of improvement?

Week Three:

Write out your goal, vision and mission.

Plan and schedule your ideal week three.

Remember to set simple goals and intentions around our tracked tasks - sleep, nutrition, exercise, work and social. Please keep it simple and avoid overloading your week with tasks and intentions.

Visualisation Exercise: Review your goal, vision and mission each morning. Include this as a task block in your daily plan.

Make a list of two not-negotiable actions for each day (these are new tasks that move you towards your goal. One of the not-negotiable tasks this week is to read your vision and mission/goal statement each morning).

Review the day's plan and adjust if needed at the start of each day. Then, track your daily activities against this plan.

The objective is to practise planning and working on a daily plan.

End of week review:

Did you track each day consistently?

Did you review your daily plan at the start of each day?

How close was your daily plan to the actual day's activities?

How often did you meet your set intentions and tasks?

Week Four:

Repeat week three. Only add new tasks and goals when you successfully and consistently execute your two not-negotiable tasks.

From here, add in an additional new task that works towards your goal and vision. Remember, we are building solid and consistent habits and rituals.

End of week four review:

Repeat as per week three reviews.

Week Five and beyond

Review week four, revise, add or adjust if needed, repeat.

A Final Word from the Author

I am a warrior to my heart. I stand in my power.

Thank you.

It is always an incredible honour knowing that someone like you has taken the time to listen to, watch or read my work. You are why I do what I do. Because I believe that you deserve to be a happy person, living a happy, meaningful and fulfilling life. I hope this book delivered everything you were seeking, and more.

I want you to know that what you want is possible – more than possible.

But what I really want you to know is that there is so much more for you beyond what you believe to be possible right now. And I want you to know that I believe it is possible for you. And if you need to, you can borrow my belief until you can truly believe it for yourself.

I can put my hand on my heart and promise you that the life I live now is far beyond what I ever imagined. And importantly, it feels like I am only just beginning to scratch the surface of the possibilities. With a growing sense of inner peace, which is for me the ultimate measure of my success.

I aim to live a good life, to show up fully, to be a decent human being, contribute, and be happy. To rest my head on the pillow at the end of each day, knowing that I have done my best.

I don't always get this right, and neither will you, and that is perfectly okay. This is what makes us human (and this is what we have The Big Guns for). What counts is that we hold the vision, keep picking ourselves up when we fall, keep showing up, learning and enjoying ourselves in the process.

Life has so much more available for us. All we have to do is choose it.

Remembering always that there is no other side, no ultimate destination. There is only here, and there is only now: learning to lean into whatever this present moment holds.

This work is ongoing, challenging and can at times feel like it is all too hard. As a result, it's tempting to think it's easier to quit as you convince yourself that things are not so bad after all. Or to beat yourself up, that it's too late and you've missed the boat (it's never too late, and you haven't).

If you've got any questions or want to share your thoughts, please email me at Fiona@thehappinesshunter.com

I would love to hear from you.

Keep believing it is possible. And keep believing it is possible for you.

Keep showing up. Just take one step forward in the general direction of your dreams, especially when you don't think you can.

Whatever it takes. No matter what.

Keep going.

I promise you it is worth it.

Fiona ♡

Acknowledgments

As with most things in life, writing a book is not a solo effort, even as so much of the time you are on your own.

To my family, especially my children, Ariston and Vivienne. Thank you for choosing me to be your mum, and for being the catalyst and the inspiration to change. It's a real delight to be able to write your names in this book and imagine your grinning faces. High five! You are two of my greatest teachers. My mum Helene, dad Mike, sister Cazz and nephew Jimmy. Thank you for being such kind people and for supporting me so much throughout my life. To Brendan and Alex. Thank you for opening up your home during such a challenging time, giving me the space to pivot without panic.

Thank you to Dora Altintas, my book writing coach, editor, publisher (and everything in between) who once again has got me over the line. What a ride. Along with starting a business, I would say that writing a book is one of the greatest personal development exercises a person can ever undertake. Thank you for helping me organise my thinking and working through what came up along the way. I'm very grateful for your guidance, patience and clever ideas. For Maria Augustus-Dunn, for your thoughtful feedback as you were proofing the copy. I'm grateful for your contribution to the process. Thank you also to

Susan High, Melinda Samson, Cynthia Merrill and Stacey Slabe for letting me know what you felt was missing, forcing me to go a level deeper. This book is better because of your honesty, and I am grateful.

Thank you Paul O'Brien for sharing what was to become The Seven Elements with me, and for all of those amazing conversations we had about the framework, Life Integration, and what it means to live it. Thank you for your generosity, for your friendship and support. I am grateful for that time we shared, the connections and opportunities created.

For everyone in The Happiness Hunter community. You are what makes The Happiness Hunter what it is. Thank you for trusting me to be your coach, joining a program, letting me into your business, listening to a podcast, leading or coming on a walk, having a healing, attending a retreat, participating in a workshop, commenting on a social media post, reading a newsletter, sending me a message, watching a video, masterclass or webinar, buying a book, booking me to speak at your event, sitting in the audience at an event, telling your friends. I hope that you enjoy this book, that it's useful and has been worth the wait.

Being in business can be so challenging and having the support of a solid network is critical to our success. Loren Bartley, what a gift you have been on this business journey. Thanks for inviting me to be part of the Business Addicts podcast: what a life-changing experience that was. To Alanna Quigley, for the brainstorming, for all of your effort, for your loyalty and your shared belief in the mission of The Happiness Hunter. And, thank you too, Mish Green. More recently, my lovely coach Bernadette Doyle from the other side of the world. You have taught me so much. So many beautiful friends, clients, colleagues, contractors, advisors, coaches, mentors, partners, podcast guests and suppliers that I've connected with along the way. Without thanking you all individually - because I don't want to miss anyone - thank you. For the risk-takers, for everyone who believed in and took action on the dream planted in their heart, and for all of the courageous women in business who I've admired, been inspired by and felt massively triggered by at times over the years. Who took the leap, backed themselves, kept going when it was really hard and didn't know how they could go on for one more day - yet did - and then willingly shared what they discovered. Thank you for showing me what is possible.

For Ruth, who so gently encouraged me to invite Jesus into my heart.

And finally, for all the lessons, thank you.

About the Author

Fiona Redding helps people become happier. She is the founder of The Happiness Hunter, a mindset coach and strategist, facilitator and speaker, creator of The Steps for Changes, producer and host of The Happiness Hunter Podcast, co-host of the Business Addicts podcast and author of The Happiness Hunter's Guide to Meditation.

She lives by the beach in Melbourne, Australia, with her children Ariston and Vivienne.

By her own admission, Fiona's journey into business has been a pretty interesting road. In many ways, and at many points, it would have made much more sense logically to just go and get a "real job".

Yet it was an unshakable faith and trust in the path she had chosen that kept her metaphorically and literally putting one foot in front of the other.

Fiona's belief in her mission and purpose continues to be rewarded in both tangible and intangible ways. With The Happiness Hunter community and walks, and a coaching, speaking and healing business, Fiona now spends her days helping others transform their lives and businesses.

www.ingramcontent.com/pod-product-compliance
Lightning Source LLC
Chambersburg PA
CBHW070248010526
44107CB00056B/2388